IDIOT'S GUIDES.

AS EASY AS IT GETS!

Canning and Preserving

by Trish Sebben-Krupka

ALPHA

A member of Penguin Group (USA) Inc.

ALPHA BOOKS

Published by Penguin Group (USA) Inc.

Penguin Group (USA) Inc., 375 Hudson Street, New York, New York 10014, USA • Penguin Group (Canada), 90 Eglinton Avenue East, Suite 700, Toronto, Ontario M4P 2Y3, Canada (a division of Pearson Penguin Canada Inc.) • Penguin Books Ltd., 80 Strand, London WC2R 0RL, England • Penguin Ireland, 25 St. Stephen's Green, Dublin 2, Ireland (a division of Penguin Books Ltd.) • Penguin Group (Australia), 250 Camberwell Road, Camberwell, Victoria 3124, Australia (a division of Pearson Australia Group Pty. Ltd.) • Penguin Books India Pvt. Ltd., 11 Community Centre, Panchsheel Park, New Delhi—110 017, India • Penguin Group (NZ), 67 Apollo Drive, Rosedale, North Shore, Auckland 1311, New Zealand (a division of Pearson New Zealand Ltd.) • Penguin Books (South Africa) (Pty.) Ltd., 24 Sturdee Avenue, Rosebank, Johannesburg 2196, South Africa • Penguin Books Ltd., Registered Offices: 80 Strand, London WC2R 0RL, England

International Standard Book Number: 978-1-61564-460-5
Library of Congress Catalog Card Number: 2013956276

16   15   14   8   7   6   5   4   3   2   1

Interpretation of the printing code: The rightmost number of the first series of numbers is the year of the book's printing; the rightmost number of the second series of numbers is the number of the book's printing. For example, a printing code of 14-1 shows that the first printing occurred in 2014.

Note: This publication contains the opinions and ideas of its author. It is intended to provide helpful and informative material on the subject matter covered. It is sold with the understanding that the author and publisher are not engaged in rendering professional services in the book. If the reader requires personal assistance or advice, a competent professional should be consulted. The author and publisher specifically disclaim any responsibility for any liability, loss, or risk, personal or otherwise, which is incurred as a consequence, directly or indirectly, of the use and application of any of the contents of this book.

Most Alpha books are available at special quantity discounts for bulk purchases for sales promotions, premiums, fund-raising, or educational use. Special books, or book excerpts, can also be created to fit specific needs. For details, write: Special Markets, Alpha Books, 375 Hudson Street, New York, NY 10014.

Trademarks: All terms mentioned in this book that are known to be or are suspected of being trademarks or service marks have been appropriately capitalized. Alpha Books and Penguin Group (USA) Inc. cannot attest to the accuracy of this information. Use of a term in this book should not be regarded as affecting the validity of any trademark or service mark.

Publisher
Mike Sanders

Executive Managing Editor
Billy Fields

Executive Acquisitions Editor
Lori Cates Hand

Development Editor
Kayla Dugger

Production Editor
Jana M. Stefanciosa

Senior Web/Graphic Designer
William Thomas

Photographer
Kevin Bertolacci

Indexer
Johnna VanHoose Dinse

Proofreader
Laura Caddell

Contents

Part 5   Jams, Jellies, and Preserves   127

Part 6   Canning Tomatoes and Tomato Products 163

Part 7   Pickling   189

Part 8   Pressure Canning   229

Appendix A   Glossary   268

Appendix B   References and Further Reading   272

Index   274

Introduction

Welcome to the wonderful world of home food preservation! Humans have been preserving food in various ways as long as we have been eating it. Our cultures have, for the most part, gone from *having* to preserve food in order to survive to *wanting* to preserve food for a variety of reasons.

Perhaps you are looking to live a locavore lifestyle, eating closer to home. Or maybe you have a large garden and have too much to give away or eat yourself. You could be concerned about pesticides and irradiation of your food. Or maybe you are a "foodie" and enjoy creating and sharing artisanal foods.

Canning and preserving allows you to have access to locally grown food throughout the year, reducing your food miles and allowing you to choose your food sources responsibly. Plus, making your own jams, jellies, and specialty foods provides a tremendous amount of pleasure in the kitchen.

How This Book Is Organized

This book is organized into eight parts. It is my hope that you will choose to read each one of them, as each passes along vital information, tips, and tricks for success. If you do choose to skip around, be sure to at the very least read Part 3 before you begin working with a boiling-water canner.

In Part 1, you'll learn everything you need to know to successfully freeze foods, and you'll explore methods for cold storage. In Part 2, I discuss dehydrating. Many people choose to dry foods due to storage constraints, or for long-term storage.

Part 3 covers the ground rules of home canning, from a basic overview of food science and safety, to steps for processing foods in a boiling-water canner. Part 4 will prepare you to put up a season's bounty of whole and sliced fruit, as well as delicious, shelf-stable fruit pie fillings.

In Part 5, you'll learn to make all kinds of gelled products, such as jams and preserves, jellies, conserves, and delicious fruit butters. Part 6 teaches you everything you need to know about tomato products. You'll can whole tomatoes, sauce, and salsa, and even make your own tomato juice.

Part 7 covers pickling. From simple quick pickles, to fermented products, to colorful relishes, fruit, and vegetable pickles, your pantry will burst with seasonal bounty. If you plan to can vegetables at home, Part 8 is required reading. Vegetables must be canned using a different process due to their low-acid nature. Pressure canning can seem intimidating, but I'll make it easy for you to get started and put up your own vegetables and tomato-vegetable mixes.

Acknowledgments

I cannot begin to express my gratitude to those who helped to make this book a reality. I must first thank my husband, best friend, and partner in life, Jim Krupka. Your endless love and support has allowed me to live my dreams, and I am forever grateful. Thanks for believing in me, and for always doing the dishes.

Special thanks are due to my agent, Marilyn Allen, of the Allen O'Shea Literary Agency. I am forever grateful to my amazing editors, Lori Cates Hand, Executive Acquisitions Editor, and Kayla Dugger, Development Editor, for their gentle guidance and encouragement throughout this process. I must also thank Kevin Bertolacci for his patience, and for taking the amazing photos, and Karyn Gerhard for her support and guidance, and for helping me to see the visual narrative of this, my first step-by-step illustrated book. I also offer my gratitude to Carole Cancler for agreeing to do the technical review of this book.

I would not have been able to write this book without the support of the amazing women who helped me in the kitchen: my sister, Kristin Doherty, and my lifelong friend, Gina Hyams. Thanks for the prep work, long days on your feet, piles of dishes, crazy errands, and "therapy sessions." Thanks are also due to my friend Karin Socaransky, for all of the beautiful old jars from her mom's basement. I must also thank my friend and mentor, Kim Donahue of Carl Schaedel and Co., Inc., for her endless support and encouragement, the long periods of time off to write and edit, as well as the use of our culinary facilities for the often chaos-inducing photo shoots for this book. Thanks are also due to the Kuehm Family of Farms View Roadstand for growing such fantastic produce and always fulfilling my "special requests", and to my dear friend Edna Brickett, whose memory lives on every time I get out my canner.

Special Thanks to the Technical Reviewer

Idiot's Guides: Canning and Preserving was reviewed by an expert who double-checked the accuracy of what you'll learn here, to help us ensure this book gives you everything you need to know about canning and preserving. Special thanks are extended to Carole Cancler.

Part 1

Freezing and Storing Food

Freezing is a simple, accessible method of food preservation. Try freezing fruits, vegetables, herbs, and prepared foods. There are lots of good reasons to freeze foods, including preserving nutrients and saving money. Plus, you'll love having a selection of fresh, convenient, and high-quality foods on hand. Don't have a big freezer? Consider setting aside part of your cellar or garage as a cold storage area. You'll be able to keep hearty vegetables fresh throughout the winter months, and you'll have the perfect cool, dark area to store your canned goods as well.

Tools and Equipment for Freezing Food

Freezing requires very little in the way of tools and equipment, making it an excellent choice for those who are new to food preservation. You may find you already have many of the following items necessary to get started.

Fresh produce

Freezing does not improve the quality or ripeness of foods, so choose produce that's perfectly ripe and ready to eat.

Freezer-safe containers

Choose durable containers that are moisture and vapor proof and resistant to cracking at low temperatures. Appropriate choices include wide-mouth canning jars (jars with narrow necks will crack when frozen food expands); glass storage containers designed for the freezer; and rigid plastic containers, such as stackable freezer jars.

Freezer bags

These should be bags designed only for use in the freezer. They must be moisture and vapor proof to keep out unwanted moisture and odors. Invest in a vacuum sealer, or simply use a straw to suck out extra air. Freezer bags can be packed with liquids or solids.

Pot or blancher

Blanching vegetables and some fruits before freezing halts the action of spoilage enzymes, resulting in better nutrient retention, flavor, and texture. You can use a pot or blancher to blanch about 1 pound (453.5 g) food at a time.

Sieve or Chinese strainer

Once food is blanched, you need to quickly remove it from the water. A long-handled sieve or Chinese strainer allows you to scoop food quickly from boiling water.

Clean kitchen towels

After foods are blanched, you will need to pat them dry to prevent ice crystals from forming on the surface. Gently roll blanched food in a clean, lint-free kitchen towel, or pat dry with paper towels.

Metal sheet pans

If you're planning to use the tray-pack method, have a few metal sheet pans lined with parchment or freezer paper ready to go.

Aluminum foil

Heavy-duty aluminum foil is appropriate for freezer use but can tear easily. If you're using aluminum foil, add an overwrap, such as a freezer bag or several layers of plastic wrap.

Freezer paper

This is moisture- and vapor-proof, heavy-duty, and grease-proof paper that's waxed on one side. Freezer paper makes a sturdy, nonstick liner for pans when you do the tray-pack method.

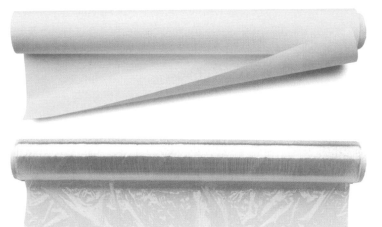

Plastic wrap

Plastic wrap makes an excellent overwrap for foods wrapped in freezer paper or aluminum foil.

Ice bath

Once foods are blanched, they need to be cooled quickly. Immediately submerge them in a bowl of ice, or—for better nutrient retention—create a "dry" ice bath (see "Steps for Freezing Food").

Sugar

Some fruits can simply be tossed with sugar and allowed to stand for 30 minutes before packing. Fruit packed in this manner will form its own syrup.

Treatment solution

Light-colored foods benefit from a dip in ascorbic (citric) acid or a commercial product, such as Fruit-Fresh, to retain freshness and color. Other foods, such as berries, don't require pretreatment. Refer to the table in each part for the specific treatment options for individual fruits and vegetables.

Simple syrup

Most fruits need a 30 percent simple syrup solution. See "Freezing Fruits" for instructions.

Freezing Basics

When freezing foods, you need to first consider the type of freezer you'll use for storing your frozen foods. You then need to think about how you'll use your frozen foods in the best and most efficient manner.

Choosing a Freezer

The freezer section of your refrigerator will not hold foods at 0°F (-18°C)—the recommended temperature to keep frozen foods fresh—and is not a good choice for long-term food storage (beyond 2 months). Plus, opening and closing the door of your refrigerator or freezer several times a day will cause temperature fluctuations that promote spoilage of frozen foods. If you want to store food for longer periods of time and have the space and the budget, a stand-alone freezer is a great investment. Freestanding freezers are available in chest and upright models. Look for an Energy Star–rated freezer to keep energy costs under control.

Upright Freezers

Upright freezers have a smaller footprint than chest freezers, and it's much easier to organize and keep track of your food. However, they are typically more expensive to purchase and run than chest freezers. While all of your frozen foods are easy to find with a quick glance, it can be difficult to store larger items without removing a shelf. If you value organization, don't relish the thought of having to dig around in a chest freezer for what you want, and have a little extra money in your budget, an upright freezer can be an excellent choice.

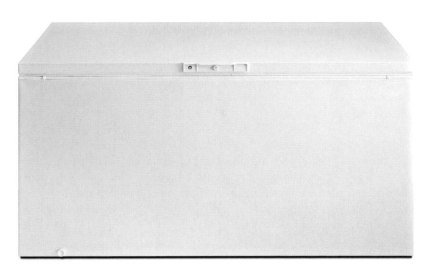

Chest Freezers

Chest freezers have a low profile and are available in many sizes, from just a few cubic feet to 25-cubic-foot+ (.7-cubic-meter) behemoths that will store an entire winter's worth of goodness. Chest freezers are well insulated, and most are defrosted manually. They are the most efficient choice, because every bit of the freezer is usable space. Organizing a chest freezer can be a challenge, though, as foods at the bottom can be difficult to reach and are sometimes lost in the shuffle.

Freezer Use and Care

When choosing a spot for your freezer, make sure it's a convenient, well-ventilated location that has good air circulation on all sides. Garages and other spaces without climate control are a poor choice for freezer placement. Instead, choose a cool, dry place where temperatures are relatively stable.

Whether you've chosen a manual-defrost or frost-free model, you also need to clean your freezer at least once a year. I like to clean mine in early spring, when I've used most of the food from the previous year, and early spring crops like peas and strawberries are still on the vine. Defrost if necessary, and use a solution of baking soda and hot water to clean the freezer inside and out.

Make sure you also keep a thermometer in your freezer to monitor the temperature. Aim to keep the temperature at or below 0°F (-18°C) to maintain quality. An easy way to monitor freezer performance is with a zipper-lock bag of ice cubes—if the ice cubes melt and refreeze, it's a sure sign your freezer is not functioning optimally.

Power Outages

If the power goes out, don't panic—and don't open the freezer door! Wrap your freezer in blankets or quilts and keep the door closed. If the power is going to be out for a few days, consider moving the contents of your freezer to a cooler packed with dry ice. Food that has been kept at or below 40°F (4°C) is safe to cook or refreeze. Food will remain frozen for longer in a full freezer.

Sanitizing Solutions

It's important to sanitize your work area before you begin a freezing project. Cleaning your kitchen is especially important when preserving food, as the growth of bacteria and other spoilers will be slowed—but not stopped—after freezing or other processing methods. The most effective sanitizer is a mixture of 1 scant teaspoon chlorine bleach to 1 quart water. This inexpensive mixture kills 99.999 percent of foodborne pathogens, such as *E. coli, listeria,* and *salmonella.* Spray all surfaces and wipe with a clean cloth. Wash any tools you will be using in hot, soapy water and, of course, wash your hands before and after each individual task.

Using Your Frozen Foods

Freezing food is easy, but using that food efficiently can be a challenge. I aim for keeping on hand a good mix of fruits, vegetables, herbs, and prepared foods so I'm never at a loss when I need a quick meal. Grab some frozen bananas and berries to whip up a quick smoothie or a few bags of vegetables and some stock to make soup in a flash. You can also toss a few cubes of frozen pesto in with hot, cooked pasta. Casseroles, soups, and many desserts freeze well and are a nutritious, low-cost alternative to takeout on busy evenings.

Here are some ways you can get the most out of your frozen foods:

Label with care: Label your frozen foods with a permanent marker. Include the contents, freeze date, expiration date, and quantity. You may also wish to add notes to indicate preparation instructions.

Aim for a full freezer, but don't pack it too tightly: You'll need to allow sufficient airflow around and between foods for optimal freezer performance. An overpacked freezer is just as inefficient as a nearly empty one.

Organize your freezer by food type: I try to keep separate shelves for fruits, vegetables, soups and stocks, and prepared foods. If you have a chest freezer, you may want to obtain plastic milk crates or shallow containers to categorize food, making it easier to find things quickly.

Maintain an inventory list: Keep the list on a chalkboard or clipboard near the freezer, or just tape your list to the door. Add foods, their freeze date, and their expiration date to the list, and cross them off as you use them. Remember the golden rule of inventory: "First In, First Out."

Once or twice a year, conduct a freezer inventory. Cross-reference your inventory list with the labeled food in your freezer, eat anything with an approaching expiration date, and throw away any food that is out of date or shows signs of spoilage.

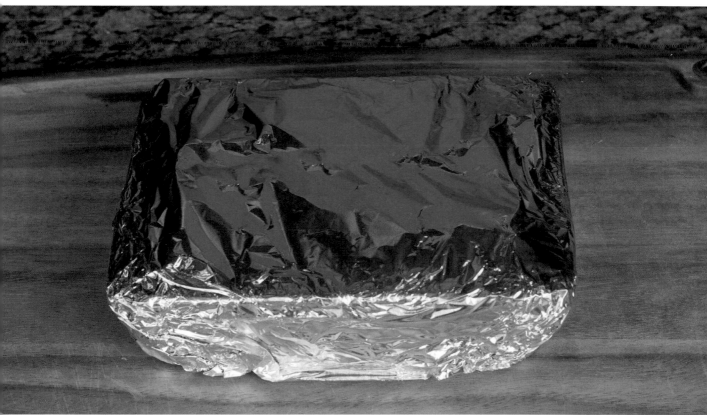

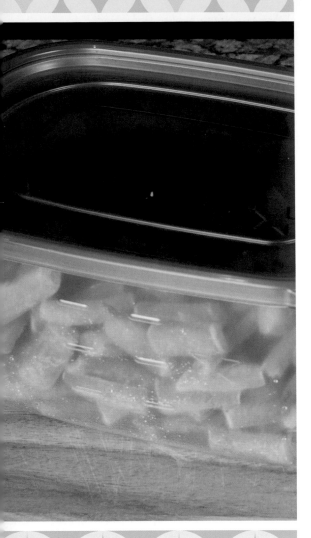

Steps for Freezing Food

Freezing food is the easiest method of food preservation. Select the freshest seasonal produce you can find.

What You'll Need

Fruits, vegetables, or herbs

Pot or blancher

Treatment solution

Sugar or simple syrup

Sheet pans

Freezer bags or rigid containers

Before You Begin

1. Sanitize your workspace.

1. Start with high-quality, fresh food

Freeze freshly harvested foods at the peak of ripeness, preferably within 24 hours of harvest. Foods that are under- or overripe will not improve in quality when frozen.

2. Wash carefully

Submerge fruits, vegetables, and herbs in plenty of cool water, and then rinse thoroughly. Molds, insect eggs, dirt, and so on should be thoroughly washed away before freezing.

3a. Blanch vegetables

Blanching helps retain vegetables' flavor, freshness, and vitamin content. Try steam blanching for the best results with the least amount of nutrient loss.

3b. Pretreat fruits

Dip fruits prone to browning in a treatment solution made with ascorbic acid, Fruit-Fresh, or lemon juice. Some can be tray packed without sugar, while others freeze best packed in a simple sugar or syrup.

Making a "Dry" Ice Bath

If you submerge food in an ice bath after blanching, some nutrients will leach out into the water, and you'll need to carefully pat it dry. For a "dry" ice bath, fill a large casserole dish with ice and place a smaller metal pan inside the dish, and make sure to have a large zipper-lock bag of ice ready. As vegetables are blanched, drain them well, transfer them to the pan, and cover with the ice blanket. Once the food is cooled, simply drain it on a clean kitchen towel and freeze.

4. Cool before freezing

For best results, chill foods in the refrigerator before freezing. Ice crystals form when food freezes slowly, creating a mushy, watery product.

5. Freeze quickly

Set your freezer at or below 0°F (-18°C) and freeze on sheet pans only 2 to 3 pounds (1 to 1.25 kg) of food per square foot or square meter of freezer space per day for best results.

6. Choose appropriate containers

Store foods packed in liquid or syrup in rigid containers. Tray-packed produce works well in plastic freezer bags. Canning jars or BPA-free plastic containers with straight sides and wide mouths are great for storing sauces and liquids.

7. Wrap tightly

When using plastic freezer bags, freezer paper, plastic wrap, or aluminum foil, wrap food tightly using several layers of material, and remove as much air as possible to reduce freezer burn or spoilage.

8. Label and keep an inventory

Use a permanent marker to label packaging with the type of food, weight or number of servings, freeze date, expiration date, and preparation instructions (if desired). Plan to use frozen foods within 8 to 12 months.

Unsuitable Freezer Containers

Don't freeze foods in bread bags, plastic bags that are not labeled for freezing, commercial glass jars (such as spaghetti sauce jars), or plastic food containers (such as those for cottage cheese or nondairy whipped topping)—these containers are not designed to be moisture and vapor proof. Glass jars can crack, and bread bags can even contaminate foods with lead! Choose appropriate packaging for both quality and safety.

9. Keep the door closed

Opening and closing the door of your freezer causes temperature fluctuations that can damage your food, so always know what you want before you open the door.

Freezing Fruits

For freezing, choose fruit that's perfectly ripe but still firm. Overripe fruit is not appropriate for any method of preservation and should be consumed immediately. Underripe fruit develops unpleasant flavors when frozen and contains enzymes that promote spoilage.

What You'll Need

Fresh fruit

Pot or blancher

Paring knife

Ice bath

Paper towels or kitchen towels

Food processor

Simple syrup or sugar

Treatment solution (such as Fruit-Fresh or an ascorbic acid-water solution)

Freezer paper

Sheet pans

Freezer bags or rigid containers

Methods for Packing Fruit

Syrup pack: For quality and sweetness, pack fruits in 30 percent simple syrup. To make a syrup, stir 1¾ cups sugar for every 4 cups water over medium heat until completely dissolved. If desired, stir in ½ teaspoon ascorbic acid per quart of syrup. Cool, and chill before using. Add ½ cup chilled syrup to each container, and fill with fruit, leaving 1 inch (2.5 cm) headspace. Cover fruit with syrup, put on lids, and freeze. Once fruit has frozen, open each container and fill with crushed waxed paper to reduce freezer burn.

Fruit juice or water pack: If you're concerned about added sugar, fruit can be packed in fruit juice or water using the same packing method as the syrup pack.

Dry tray pack: The dry tray–pack method allows you to freeze fruits individually before putting them into a container. This method is fantastic for berries, as you can open the container, scoop out a cup or two, and return the container to the freezer without the contents sticking together. If you are tray packing whole fruits, simply wash, dry, and pit or peel if necessary. You then spread fruits on freezer paper–lined sheet pans, and freeze. Once fruit has frozen, transfer it to freezer bags, and remove extra air by folding the bag or sucking out the air with a straw. Label the bags, and return them immediately to the freezer.

Sugar pack: Unsweetened fruits lose their quality more quickly than those packed in syrup or sugar. Fruits not packed in syrup may be sprinkled with sugar (about ¾ cup per quart of fruit). To do this, toss and stir fruit until sugar melts and juices are drawn out and then pack the fruit into containers.

1. Wash
Wash fruit in plenty of cold, running water. Trim away soft spots or blemishes.

2. Blanch and/or peel
Refer to "Best Methods for Freezing Fruits" table to see whether fruit should be blanched before peeling.

Blanch in boiling water, pit and peel if necessary, and chill using the ice bath or "dry" ice bath method (see "Steps for Freezing Food"). Pat dry with paper towels or clean kitchen towels.

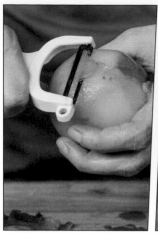

3. Slice or purée

Cut larger fruits into uniform pieces. Sort smaller whole fruits by size. Softer fruits, such as avocados and bananas, can be puréed.

4. Treat

Use one of the four methods in the "Methods for Packing Fruit" sidebar to prepare fruit for packing. If desired, treat fruits that may darken with a treatment solution.

5. Freeze quickly

Set your freezer at or below 0°F (-18°C) and freeze on sheet pans only 2 to 3 pounds (1 to 1.25 kg) of food per square foot or square meter of freezer space per day for best results.

6. Pack

Pack fruit. Transfer to rigid containers (for sugar-packed fruits and fruits frozen in syrup, water, or juice) or freezer bags (tray-packed fruit). Use within 1 year.

Best Methods for Freezing Fruits

Fruit	Preparation	Pack
Apples	Wash, peel, and slice.	Pack in 30 percent syrup with ½ tsp. ascorbic acid per qt. syrup or Fruit-Fresh per package instructions.
Apricots, peaches, or nectarines	Wash, and blanch for 1 minute. Peel, pit, and slice.	Syrup pack, or treat with ascorbic acid and then dry tray pack.
Avocados	Peel, mash, and add ⅛ tsp. ascorbic acid per 1 qt. purée.	Pack in freezer-safe containers in serving-size portions.
Bananas	Peel, treat, and cut into chunks or mash.	Tray pack chunks, or pack purée in serving-size portions.
Berries	Wash and dry on clean kitchen towels.	Tray pack, sugar pack, or syrup pack.
Cherries	Wash, pit, and dry.	Sugar pack with ¾ cup sugar per qt.
Citrus	Wash, peel, and segment.	Syrup pack or fruit juice pack with ½ tsp. ascorbic acid per qt.
Grapes	Wash and separate individual grapes.	Dry tray pack whole grapes.
Pears	Wash, peel, and slice.	Syrup pack with ½ tsp. ascorbic acid per qt. syrup.
Plums	Wash and pit.	Syrup pack with ½ tsp. ascorbic acid per qt. syrup.
Rhubarb	Wash, cut, and blanch for 2 minutes.	Tray pack or syrup pack.

Freezing Vegetables

Freezing doesn't improve the quality of vegetables, so choose tender, young, firm vegetables and freeze them as soon as they are harvested. Aim for "field to freezer" in less than 24 hours for best results.

What You'll Need

Vegetables

Paring knife

Pot or blancher

Ice bath

Kitchen towel or paper towels

Freezer paper

Sheet pans

Freezer bags or rigid containers

1. Wash
Wash freshly harvested vegetables in plenty of cold, running water.

2. Cut and trim
If necessary, cut vegetables into bite-sized pieces. Trim away any blemishes or soft spots.

Methods for Blanching

Water blanching: Using 1 gallon (3.75 L) boiling water, blanch 1 pound (453.5 g) vegetables at a time. With this ratio, the water should continue to boil when the vegetables are added.

Steam blanching: Steam blanching is recommended for grated vegetables (such as summer squash), broccoli, sweet potatoes, and other delicate vegetables that might become mushy when immersed in boiling water. To do this, fit a pot with a tight-fitting lid with a steamer basket insert, and bring 1 to 2 inches (2.5 to 5 cm) water to a boil. Blanch 1 pound (453.5 g) vegetables at a time. Steam blanching takes a bit longer than water blanching, but the improvement in quality is often worth the extra time.

Microwave blanching: Microwave blanching is not recommended. Research has shown that some enzymes that promote spoilage remain active using this type of blanching. The food also cooks at different rates, causing mushy, uneven results. In addition, this method will not save time or energy.

3. Blanch
Refer to the "Best Methods for Freezing Vegetables" table to determine the method and blanching time for each particular vegetable.

4. Cool
After blanching, immediately cool vegetables using an ice bath or the "dry" ice method (see "Steps for Freezing Food").

5. Roll or pat dry
Quickly dry blanched and cooled vegetables by gently rolling them in a clean kitchen towel or patting them dry with paper towels.

6. Freeze quickly
Set your freezer at or below 0°F (-18°C) and freeze on sheet pans only 2 to 3 pounds (1 to 1.25 kg) of food per square foot or square meter of freezer space per day for best results.

7. Pack
For best results, use the tray-pack method. Spread vegetables on freezer paper–lined sheet pans, and freeze. Transfer to freezer bags or rigid containers. You may also dry pack the prepared vegetables directly in containers. Use within 1 year.

Best Methods for Freezing Vegetables

Vegetable	Preparation	Blanching Method and Time
Asparagus	Trim. Leave whole, or cut into 2-in. (5-cm) sections.	Water blanch large spears for 4 minutes, medium spears for 3 minutes, and small spears for 2 minutes.
Beans (pod)	Shell and sort by size.	Water blanch large beans for 4 minutes, medium beans for 3 minutes, and small beans for 2 minutes.
Beans (vine)	Trim. Cut if desired.	Water blanch for 3 minutes.
Beets	Trim and scrub.	Cook in boiling water until tender, 25 minutes.
Broccoli	Separate into florets. Immerse in salt water (4 tsp. salt per 1 gal. [3.75 L] water)	Steam blanch for 5 minutes.
Brussels sprouts	Trim. Soak as for broccoli.	Water blanch for 5 minutes.
Cabbage	Cut into shreds or wedges.	Water blanch for 1½ minutes.
Carrots	Peel. Leave whole for small carrots, or cut.	Water blanch whole carrots for 5 minutes and cut carrots for 2 minutes.
Cauliflower	Soak and trim as for broccoli. Add 2 tsp. lemon juice to blanching water to prevent darkening.	Water blanch 3 minutes, with 2 tsp. lemon juice added to water to prevent darkening.
Corn	Husk and trim. To freeze whole-kernel corn, blanch on the cob, cool, then remove kernels.	For corn on the cob, blanch for 7 minutes. For corn kernels, blanch for 4 minutes; cool, and remove kernels.
Peas (edible pod)	Remove stems, blossom ends, and strings.	Water blanch for 2 minutes.
Peas (green or field)	Shell.	Water blanch for 1½ to 2 minutes.
Peppers (hot)	Roast or steam. Peel.	No blanching required.
Peppers (sweet)	Halve or cut into strips.	Freeze without blanching (if serving raw), or water blanch for 2 minutes (for cooked preparations).
Pumpkin, squash (winter), and sweet potatoes	Cut and remove seeds.	Steam or cook in boiling water until tender.
Squash (summer)	Wash and slice.	Steam blanch for 3 minutes.
Tomatoes	Core. Peel after blanching.	Water blanch for 30 seconds, and then peel.
Turnips/parsnips	Peel and cube.	Water blanch for 3 minutes.

Freezing Herbs

Leafy herbs—such as basil, parsley, chervil, and chives—are the best choice for freezing. Remember, frozen herbs cannot be used for garnish; they become limp once frozen.

What You'll Need

Herbs

Salad spinner or kitchen towels

Freezer paper

Freezer bags

Ice cube trays or freezer containers

Water or olive oil

Herb Mixture Warning

Garlic or herb vinegars and oils are considered hazardous due to the presence of bacteria like botulism and *E. coli,* which are activated in an anaerobic environment (such as when submerged in oil). The U.S. FDA requires commercially prepared garlic-infused mixtures to contain bacterial inhibitors to prevent the growth of bacteria and recommends fresh preparation only for home use. Oil or vinegar mixtures with herbs should be consumed within 3 days, or frozen immediately. To play it safe, add garlic to herb mixtures just before using, and consume within 1 to 2 days.

1. Wash herbs

Wash herbs carefully in several changes of cold water, and dry in a salad spinner or between layers of clean kitchen towels. Use any of the following steps to freeze herbs.

2a. Wrap

Place herbs in a single layer between pieces of freezer paper, and pack in freezer bags.

2b. Pack in water

Finely chop herbs, and mix with a few tablespoons of water or olive oil to form a dense paste. Pack into ice cube trays or freezer containers.

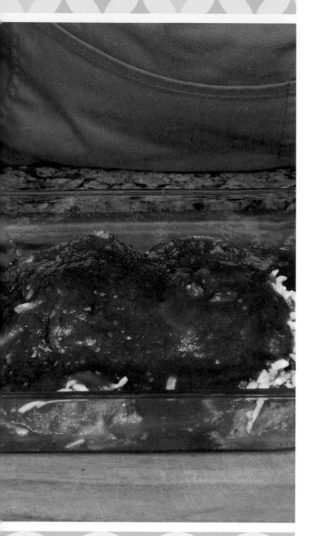

Freezing Prepared Foods

Casseroles, soups, stews, pasta sauces, and stocks freeze well. Plus, it's nice to have a few meals planned out and ready to go in the freezer. When using frozen prepared foods, defrost them in the refrigerator overnight, or simply cook frozen foods over low heat or in the oven. Always insulate prepared foods with several layers of wrap to prevent freezer burn.

What You'll Need

Prepared food

Plastic wrap or freezer paper

Heavy-duty aluminum foil

Rigid containers or jars

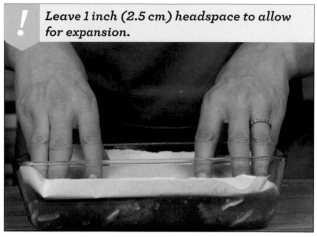

Leave 1 inch (2.5 cm) headspace to allow for expansion.

1. Prepare food

Cook stock, sauce, or soup according to the recipe, undercooking slightly to compensate for reheating. Assemble casseroles with cooked components, but do not bake. Cool for 30 minutes, and then refrigerate for 2 to 3 hours until completely chilled.

2. Pack

Pack soups, stews, sauces, and stocks in rigid plastic containers or wide-mouth canning jars. Pack unbaked casseroles in the dish you will use for baking. Freeze, then cover the surface of the food with plastic wrap or freezer paper, and fill the air space with crumpled waxed paper or freezer paper to eliminate air and prevent freezer burn.

3. Wrap and label

Put on lid or wrap top in aluminum foil. Label all prepared foods with the contents, serving size, and date frozen. Use within 3 months.

Seasonings in Prepared Foods

Some seasonings can develop stronger flavors or fade into the background when frozen. Seasonings that change in flavor include salt and sugar substitutes, curry powder, sage, celery, pepper, cloves, and raw garlic. Leave these seasonings out of dishes intended for the freezer; you can add them before heating, if desired. Be sure to label the container with the missing ingredients before freezing.

Cellaring Foods in Cold Storage

If you have a well-ventilated basement or shed, you can successfully cellar cool-weather crops. The keys to successful cellaring are temperature, light, and humidity control. A cool, dark space with a window for ventilation is the best choice.

Good choices for cellaring include pears, apples, persimmons, onions, garlic, potatoes, winter squash, sweet potatoes, parsnips, and pumpkins. Pick late-season tomatoes while still green, and ripen in storage.

What You'll Need

Milk crates or boxes
Pack crates about a quarter full for best results. One spoiled apple, onion, or potato can ruin the whole box, so it's best not to "put all your eggs in one basket."

Packing materials
These allow for airflow, absorb excess humidity, and prevent damage. Separate layers of produce with newspaper or cardboard, or use burlap sacks for vegetables such as potatoes, which must be stored in complete darkness.

Shelves
If your space doesn't have built-in shelving, inexpensive shelves from the hardware store or a flea market are a great choice.

Fan
Use a fan to bring in cool air to a warm room or expel cool air from a cold room.

Storing Fruits and Vegetables

Choose separate storage areas for vegetables and fruits. Certain fruits, such as apples, figs, pears, plums, and tomatoes, give off ethylene gas, which causes potatoes to sprout and onions to spoil.

Strong-smelling vegetables—such as cabbages, rutabagas, and turnips—are a poor choice for in-home root cellaring. To avoid those odors, store these vegetables in the garage or other outdoor root cellar.

Cooler Storage

If your only option is the garage and you live in a region with very cold temperatures, large insulated coolers can be a good choice for cellaring. Pack hardy vegetables or fruits—such as apples, potatoes, garlic, onions, and pears—in their own individual coolers with plenty of packing materials, and prop the lids open slightly for ventilation. Rotate produce stored in this manner on a regular basis for best results.

1. Condition
Foods with a hard shell, such as pumpkins, should be brought inside for a few days to allow their shells to harden before storing. Carefully trim stems, as breakage will accelerate spoilage.

2. Examine and pack
Remove insects and produce that shows any signs of spoilage, such as soft spots. Pack in milk crates, baskets, or boxes with holes cut in the sides.

3. Store
Place in the root cellar, and use a fan to circulate air and remove ethylene gas. Aim to keep your root cellar between 35°F and 55°F (2°C and 13°C).

Part 2

Drying Food

Drying or dehydrating preserves food by removing moisture to prevent spoilage and the growth of microorganisms. This easy, ancient form of food preservation can be useful when storage space is at a premium, as dried foods take up less space than their fresh counterparts. Dehydrated foods are long-lasting, easy to prepare, and lightweight.

Drying Whole and Sliced Fruits

Dehydrating does not improve food quality, so choose perfectly ripe, firm, and unblemished fruit. Fruit that has been sitting around too long will dehydrate poorly and be prone to spoilage, so get it into the dehydrator as soon as you pick it or arrive home from the farmers' market!

What You'll Need

Fruit

Treatment solution

Paring knife

Pot or blancher

Ice bath

Plastic or glass storage containers

Heavy-duty storage bags

Before You Begin

1. Wash
Wash fruit well to remove bacteria, molds, and insects.

2. Prepare treatment solution
If you are drying a fruit prone to browning, such as pears and apples, prepare a treatment solution. Use a commercial product, such as Fruit-Fresh, or add 1 crushed 500 mg vitamin C tablet or ¼ cup bottled lemon juice to 1 gallon (3.75 L) water.

1. Peel or check skins
Peel fruit with thicker skins. For whole, skin-on fruits or larger pieces, check the skins by piercing them in a few places with a sharp knife, or slice in half.

2. Blanch and pretreat
Blanch fruit in plenty of boiling water, and cool immediately in an ice bath. Peel and pit if necessary, and cut or slice into uniform pieces. Fruit may be pretreated with treatment solution.

3. Dry
Arrange fruit in a single layer on drying trays. Dry at 125°F to 135°F (52°C to 57°C) until most of moisture has been removed but fruit remains pliable, about 12 to 16 hours (sliced fruit) and up to 24 hours (whole fruit).

4. Condition
Cool. Pack loosely into large plastic or glass containers, and seal tightly. Shake or stir once a day; if any moisture appears, return fruits to the dehydrator until they have dehydrated sufficiently, and repeat the process.

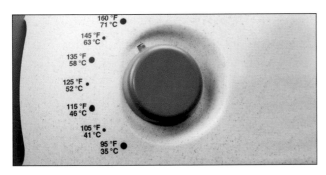

5. Pasteurize
Pasteurize dried foods in your dehydrator or oven at 160°F (71°C) for 30 minutes, or freeze at or below 0°F (-17.75°C) for 48 hours.

6. Pack and store
Cool fruit completely before storing. Pack tightly without crushing in glass or plastic containers or heavy-duty storage bags. Dried fruits can be stored for up to 1 year.

Drying Whole and Sliced Fruits

Drying Berries

Berries are easy to dry, and the results are delicious! Pack dried berries as a portable, nutritious snack, or mix them into baked goods. Dehydrated berries can also be rehydrated to make delicious jam or fruit fillings.

What You'll Need

Fruit

Antioxidant dip or treatment solution

Needle or skewer

Drying trays

Plastic or glass storage containers

Heavy-duty storage bags

Before You Begin

1. Wash
Wash fruits well to remove bacteria, molds, and insects.

2. Prepare treatment solution
Use a commercial product, such as Fruit-Fresh, or add 1 crushed 500 mg vitamin C tablet or ¼ cup bottled lemon juice to 1 gallon (3.75 L) water.

1. Pretreat and check skins

If desired, treat berries with an antioxidant dip or treatment solution. Prick firm berries, such as cranberries, with a sharp needle or skewer to check the skins. You can dry very small fruit, such as blueberries, without checking.

2. Dry

Arrange berries in single layers on drying trays. Dry at 125°F to 140°F (52°C to 60°C) until most of the moisture has been removed but berries remain pliable, about 12 hours.

3. Condition

Cool. Pack loosely into large plastic or glass containers, and seal tightly. Shake or stir once a day; if any moisture appears, return berries to the dehydrator until they have dehydrated sufficiently, and repeat the process.

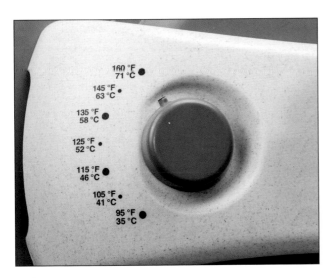

4. Pasteurize

Pasteurize berries in your dehydrator or oven at 160°F (71°C) for 30 minutes, or freeze in your freezer at or below 0°F (-17.75°C) for 48 hours.

5. Pack and store

Cool berries completely before storing. Pack tightly without crushing in glass or plastic containers or heavy-duty storage bags. Use within 1 year.

Making Fruit Leathers

Fruit leather is simply a purée of fruit mixed with optional sweetener and dried to a dense, chewy "leather." Fruit leathers can be made from both fresh and home-canned fruit. Try apples, pears, peaches, berries, grapes, citrus fruits, cherries, or bananas.

What You'll Need

Fruit

Treatment solution

Paring knife

Double boiler

Blender or food mill

Large, heavy-bottomed saucepan

Fruit leather tray or freezer paper-lined drying trays

Cornstarch

Waxed paper or freezer paper

Plastic wrap

Before You Begin

1. Wash
Wash fruits well to remove bacteria, molds, and insects.

2. Prepare treatment solution
If you are drying a fruit prone to browning, such as pears and apples, prepare a treatment solution. Use a commercial product, such as Fruit-Fresh, or add 1 crushed 500 mg vitamin C tablet or ¼ cup bottled lemon juice to 1 gallon (3.75 L) water.

1. Pit and peel
Pit fruits if necessary, peel if desired, and cut into small pieces. Treat fruits that are prone to browning with treatment solution if desired.

2. Cook (optional)
In a double boiler set over boiling water, cook fruit for 10 minutes.

3. Purée
In a blender or food mill, purée fruit until smooth.

4. Reduce purée (optional)
Pour purée into a large, heavy-bottomed saucepan, and reduce until mixture is thick and much of the liquid has evaporated, up to 1 hour. Stir frequently.

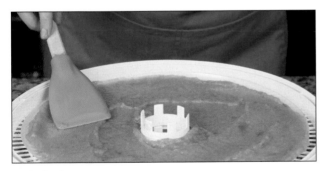

5. Dehydrate
Spread purée no more than $1/4$ inch (.75 cm) thick on fruit leather trays or freezer paper-lined drying trays. Dry at 140°F (60°C) until fruit leather feels a little tacky toward the center but moisture has been removed, about 12 hours.

6. Wrap and store
Cool completely. Brush fruit leather with a little cornstarch to prevent sticking. Place between layers of waxed paper or freezer paper, roll up, and wrap tightly in plastic wrap. Use fruit leather within 6 months.

Drying Vegetables

You have many different options for drying vegetables. Carrots, celery, onions, and potatoes are great choices for dehydrating, as they are easily rehydrated to create a flavorful base for soups and sauces. Garlic and peppers can be pulverized or flaked in a blender once dry for homemade seasoning flakes and powders (no need to blanch them first). And zucchini and carrots make excellent chips.

What You'll Need

Vegetables

Paring knife

Pot or blancher

Paper towels or kitchen towel

Plastic or glass storage containers

Heavy-duty storage bags or jars

Before You Begin

1. Wash
Wash vegetables well to remove bacteria, molds, and insects.

2. Cut
Cut vegetables into small, uniform pieces.

> **!** **Refer to the "Basic Methods for Drying Vegetables" table.**

1. Blanch

Water: Use 1 gallon (3.75 L) boiling water.

Steam: In a pot with a tight-fitting lid and a steamer basket insert, bring 1 to 2 inches (2.5 to 5 cm) water to a boil.

2. Pat dry

Use paper towels or a clean kitchen towel to press as much water out of blanched, cooled vegetables as possible.

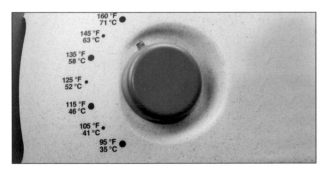

3. Dehydrate

Arrange vegetables in a single layer on drying trays. Dry at 130°F to 140°F (54°C to 60°C) until vegetables are dry and crisp, about 12 hours.

4. Condition

Cool. Pack loosely into large glass or plastic containers, and seal tightly. Shake or stir once a day; if any moisture appears, return vegetables to the dehydrator until they have dehydrated sufficiently, and repeat the process.

5. Pasteurize

Pasteurize vegetables in your dehydrator or oven at 160°F (71°C) for 30 minutes, or freeze in your freezer at or below 0°F (-17.75°C) for 48 hours.

6. Pack and store

Cool dried vegetables completely before storing. Pack tightly without crushing in glass or plastic containers, heavy-duty storage bags, or jars. Use within 1 year.

Basic Methods for Drying Vegetables

Vegetable	Preparation	Blanching Method/Time
Asparagus	Trim and cut into 2-in. (5-cm) slices.	Steam: 4 to 5 minutes Water: 3 minutes
Beans (pod)	Shell and wash well.	Steam: 3 minutes Water: 4 minutes
Beans (vine)	Trim and cut into short pieces.	Steam: 2½ minutes Water: 2 minutes
Beets	Trim and scrub. Cut into ⅛-in. (.25-cm) matchsticks after cooking.	Water: 25 minutes
Broccoli	Separate into florets. Immerse in salt water (4 tsp. salt/1 gal. water) to remove insects. Cut as for serving, and quarter stems.	Steam: 3½ minutes Water: 2 minutes
Brussels sprouts	Trim and cut in half lengthwise.	Steam: 7 minutes Water: 6 minutes
Carrots	Peel. Cut into slices or strips ⅛ in. (.25 cm) thick.	Steam: 3½ minutes Water: 3 minutes
Cauliflower	Soak and trim as for broccoli.	Steam: 4 minutes Water: 3 minutes If desired, add 1 tsp. lemon juice to water to prevent darkening.
Corn	Husk and trim. Cut kernels from the cob after blanching.	Steam: 5 minutes Water: 4 minutes
Garlic	Peel and thinly slice.	No blanching required.
Onions	Trim. Slice or chop.	No blanching required.

Vegetable	Preparation	Blanching Method/Time
Peas (edible pod)	Remove stems, blossom ends, and strings. Cut into 1/8-in. (.25-cm) strips.	Steam: 3 minutes Water: 2 minutes
Peas (green or field)	Shell.	Steam: 3 minutes Water: 2 minutes
Peppers (chile)	Wash well. Dry small peppers whole; cut larger peppers into strips.	No blanching required.
Peppers (sweet)	Wash well. Chop or cut into strips.	No blanching required.
Potatoes and turnips/parsnips	Scrub and peel. Cut into shoestrings or 1/8-in. (.25-cm) slices.	Steam: 7 minutes Water: 5 minutes
Pumpkin, squash (winter), and sweet potatoes	Peel, seed, and cut into 1/8-in. (.25-cm) slices.	Steam: 3 minutes Water: 1 minute
Squash (summer), such as zucchini, pattypan, or yellow squash	Trim and cut into 1/4-in. (.5-cm) slices.	Steam: 2 1/2 minutes Water: 1 1/2 minutes

Vegetable Drying Cautions

Vegetables contain less acid than fruit, so they must be dried until they are brittle. When only 10 percent of the moisture remains, spoilers cannot grow, and food is safe to consume. Vegetables also lose flavor and tenderness when dried; the longer the drying time, the more pronounced this effect will be. Therefore, make sure to cut vegetables into very small pieces to speed the drying times and minimize the loss of flavor and texture.

Sun-Dried Tomatoes

Drying tomatoes concentrates their flavor and sweetness, allowing you to enjoy the bright, intense flavor of freshly picked tomatoes year-round. Choose ripe, meaty plum tomatoes. Before using sun-dried tomatoes, rehydrate them in hot water or slice, cover with oil, and refrigerate overnight.

What You'll Need

Tomatoes

Paring knife

Pot or blancher

Ice bath

Plastic or glass storage containers

Heavy-duty storage bags or jars

Before You Begin

1. Wash
Wash tomatoes well to remove bacteria, molds, and insects.

2. Trim
Trim soft spots and blemishes, and cut a small x in the bottom of each tomato to prepare for blanching.

1. Blanch and peel
Blanch tomatoes in 1-pound (453.5-g) batches in at least 1 gallon (3.75 L) boiling water. Cool in an ice bath, and peel.

2. Cut and seed
Halve tomatoes, or cut into slices. Squeeze gently to remove most of the seeds.

3. Dehydrate
Dry tomatoes at 140°F (60°C) until they are leathery, with no pockets of moisture, about 12 to 16 hours.

4. Condition
Cool. Pack loosely into large plastic or glass containers, and seal tightly. Shake or stir once a day; if any moisture appears, return tomatoes to the dehydrator until they have dehydrated sufficiently, and repeat.

5. Pack and store
Cool sun-dried tomatoes completely before storing. Pack tightly without crushing in glass or plastic containers, heavy-duty storage bags, or jars. Use within 1 year.

Packing in Oil

Sun-dried tomatoes and garlic packed in oil are available on store shelves everywhere, and making them at home seems like a great idea, right? Wrong! Garlic can harbor botulism spores, which thrive in the airless environment of an oil pack. Adding herbs can also introduce dangerous spoilers. If you'd like to pack sun-dried tomatoes in oil, do so without any added herbs, garlic, or spices, and store them in the refrigerator.

Drying Chiles

Anyone who has planted chile peppers knows that you will grow more than you can use in a season. Drying a bumper crop of chiles is easy, and since you'll be drying them whole, you won't have as many worries about volatile oils burning your skin.

What You'll Need

Chiles

Paring knife

Plastic or glass storage containers

Heavy-duty storage bags or jars

Before You Begin

1. Wash
Wash chiles in plenty of cold, running water.

2. Trim and check skins
For small peppers, check the skins by making a $^1/_2$-inch (1.25-cm) slit with a sharp knife, and dry whole. Larger peppers should be halved, seeded, and sliced.

1. Dehydrate
Dry chiles at 140°F (60°C) until they are leathery, with no pockets of moisture, about 12 to 16 hours.

2. Condition
Cool. Pack loosely into large plastic or glass containers, and seal tightly. Shake or stir once a day; if any moisture appears, return chiles to the dehydrator until they have dehydrated sufficiently, and repeat the process.

3. Pasteurize
Pasteurize dried chiles in your dehydrator or oven at 160°F (71°C) for 30 minutes, or freeze in a freezer at or below 0°F (-17.75°C) for 48 hours.

4. Pack and store
Cool chiles completely before storing. Pack tightly without crushing in glass or plastic containers, heavy-duty storage bags, or jars. Use within 1 year.

Air-Drying Chiles

If you live in an environment where the relative humidity is consistently below 60 percent and the average daily temperatures are above 90°F (32°C), it's safe to air-dry chiles. Allow freshly harvested chiles to sit at room temperature for a few days to allow the stems to dry out. Tie small bunches together, three chiles at a time, and then string together those bunches in large clusters (known as *ristras*) using string or wire. Hang in a warm, dry place.

Drying Corn

It's much more common to preserve corn by freezing or canning, but if storage space is at a premium, dehydrating can be a good choice. Once dry, it can be ground into corn meal, or rehydrated. Rehydrated corn will have a different texture than fresh or frozen corn. Try it as an ingredient in soups or casseroles.

What You'll Need

Corn

Pot or blancher

Cutting board or Bundt pan

Corn cutter or sharp knife

Plastic or glass storage containers or jars

Heavy-duty storage bags

Before You Begin

1. Wash
Wash corn in plenty of cold, running water.

2. Husk and trim
Be sure to remove all traces of corn silk when husking, and trim as for corn on the cob.

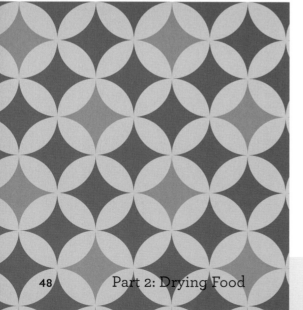

1. Blanch
Steam blanch for 5 to 6 minutes, or boiling-water blanch for 4 minutes.

2. Cut
Rest flat end of the cob on your cutting board or Bundt pan, and cut kernels away from the cob using a corn cutter or sharp knife.

3. Dehydrate
Dry corn at 130°F to 140°F (54°C to 60°C) until crisp and brittle, about 12 to 16 hours.

4. Condition
Pack in large plastic or glass storage containers or jars, and seal tightly. Shake or stir once a day for a week; if moisture appears, return corn to dehydrator until completely dry.

5. Pack and store
Cool corn completely before storing. Pack tightly in glass or plastic containers, heavy-duty storage bags, or jars. Use within 1 year.

Making Popcorn

If you grow your own corn, you can make your own popcorn, too! Corn must be dried on the stalks before harvesting, and then air-dried in a humidity-free environment below 130°F (54°C). If you're planting corn for popcorn, choose a variety that is suited to this use, such as Japanese Hull-less, Dynamite, Hybrid South American Mushroom, White Cloud, or Creme Puff. Check with your local agricultural extension or government service organization to see which varieties of corn are suited to your geographic region.

Drying Beans and Peas

The easiest way to dry beans and legumes (such as black, kidney, lima, pinto, cranberry, or black-eyed peas) is to allow them to field dry. Just leave the beans in their pods in the garden until they rattle when the pod is shaken. Then pick, shell, condition, pasteurize, and store—no pretreatment necessary. If beans show any sign of moisture during conditioning, finish drying them in the dehydrator or in your oven on the lowest setting.

Garden peas must be blanched and dried in a dehydrator for best results. You may also use the following method for beans and legumes that have not been field dried—just increase the blanching time by 2 minutes.

What You'll Need

Peas or beans

Pot or blancher

Ice bath

Colander or kitchen towels

Plastic or glass storage containers

Heavy-duty storage bags or jars

Before You Begin

1. Shell peas or beans
Shelling is a time-consuming process, so enlist a friend or family member to help!

2. Wash
Wash peas or beans after shelling to remove dirt and contaminants.

1. Blanch
Steam blanch peas for 2 minutes, or blanch in boiling water for 3 minutes. Blanch beans in boiling water for 4 minutes. Cool in an ice bath.

2. Dry
Dry peas or beans in a colander or on several layers of clean kitchen towels to remove excess water and speed dehydration.

3. Dehydrate
Dry peas or beans at 130°F to 140°F (54°C to 60°C) until they are completely dry and rattle when shaken in your hand, about 8 to 14 hours.

4. Condition
Cool. Pack loosely into large plastic or glass containers, and seal tightly. Shake or stir once a day; if any moisture appears, return peas or beans to the dehydrator until they have dehydrated sufficiently, and repeat the process.

5. Pack and store
Cool peas or beans completely before storing. Pack tightly in glass or plastic containers, heavy-duty storage bags, or jars. Use within 1 year.

Air-Drying Herbs

Herbs are one of the easiest foods to dry. They are also much cheaper and more flavorful than store-bought dried herbs. Gather herbs in the early morning in order to minimize bruising and wilting, and keep drying out of the sun for best results. Sturdy herbs, such as sage, rosemary, parsley, summer savory, and thyme, are excellent choices for air-drying.

What You'll Need

Herbs

Kitchen twine

Paper bags

Glass jars

1. Wash
Wash herbs in several changes of cold water to ensure they are clean and insect free.

2. Tie and hang
Tie herbs in bunches with kitchen twine, and hang in a warm, dry place out of direct sunlight. For tender herbs, suspend herb bunch inside a bag. Use a bag with handles, or punch holes in a paper lunch sack.

3. Store
Once herbs have dried completely, remove the leaves from the stems, and store in tightly sealed glass jars. Use within 1 year.

Herb Blends

I love to mix complementary herbs and tie them together in bundles to make herb blends. Once they've dried, I stem them and pack them in little glass jars with handwritten labels. A few little jars of your own custom herb blends are great to have on hand in the kitchen, and they make a terrific holiday hostess gift.

Try any of the following herb blends:

Poultry	Seafood	Italian	Provençal
Thyme	Chervil	Oregano	Tarragon
Tarragon	Parsley	Thyme	Parsley
Sage	Tarragon	Basil	Thyme
		Rosemary	Fennel fronds

Drying Herbs in a Dehydrator

Tender herbs, such as basil, chervil, lemon balm, verbena, and mints, have high moisture content and are best when dried quickly. You can use a dehydrator to easily accomplish this task.

What You'll Need

Herbs

Paper towel

Jars

Before You Begin

1. Wash

Wash herbs well in several changes of cold water. Check to be sure no soil or insects are clinging to the leaves. Carefully dry herbs by rolling in a paper towel.

1. Place on drying trays

Place herbs with their stems attached on drying trays.

2. Dehydrate, discard stems, pack, and store

Dry at 95°F to 115°F (35°C to 46°C) until herbs crumble when rubbed between your fingers, about 6 hours. Remove leaves from stems, discarding stems. Package herbs in tightly sealed jars. Use within 1 year.

Harvesting Fresh Herbs

Instead of waiting until the end of the season, harvest herbs continually to encourage new growth. Snip off no more than one third of the stalk's length. For leafy herbs, such as parsley and basil, pinch back at the point where the leaves divide. Chives and lavender should be cut all the way back to the soil line when harvesting. Cilantro is the only herb I've grown that does not stand up to successive harvesting. When you need a bunch of cilantro, you'll have to pick the whole plant, or it will go to seed immediately.

Early morning is the best time to harvest herbs. The dew that collected overnight has dried, but the sun has not yet baked away the essential oils near the plant's surface.

Drying Seeds

Seeds, such as sunflower and pumpkin seeds, are easily dried at home. Remember that drying and roasting are two different processes, so if you want roasted seeds, you'll need to do that after they're dried. Herb seeds, such as coriander and fennel, can be dried using this method as well.

What You'll Need

Seeds

Cheesecloth

Heavy-duty storage bags
or glass jars

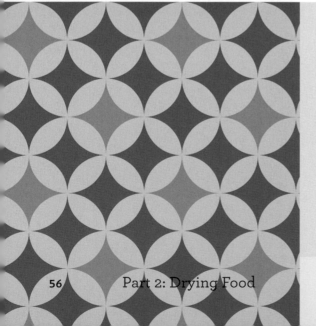

Be a Seed Saver!

If you grow tomatoes, peppers, or herbs in your garden, you may want to save the seeds for next year's planting season. You can do this with organic fruits and vegetables and any herb (except cilantro). Choose the hardiest specimens for this purpose. Scrape seeds from tomatoes or peppers, rinse them in a colander, and place on a ceramic or glass plate until dry. To save herb seeds, allow the herbs to form seeds while still on the plant, wrap in cheesecloth as for sunflower seeds, and hang in a dry place until the seeds remove themselves from the plant.

For sunflower seeds

1. Secure with cheesecloth
When seeds are visible and flowers begin to die, tie cheesecloth over flowers to keep birds from eating the seeds. The seeds will drop out on their own when they are sufficiently dry.

2. Dry
Dry seeds have no moisture left and rattle in your hand. You may also remove sunflower seeds from flowers with a spoon, and dry in a dehydrator at 100°F (38°C) for about 8 hours.

3. Store
Remove seeds, and store in heavy-duty storage bags or glass jars. For best results, keep jars or bags in the freezer or a cool room with temperatures below 55°F (13°C). Use within 1 year.

For pumpkin seeds

1. Wash
Wash pumpkin seeds well to remove all fibrous material.

2. Dehydrate
Dry pumpkin seeds in a single layer in a dehydrator or the oven at 115°F (46°C) until crisp and dry, about 10 hours in the dehydrator. If using the oven, stir seeds frequently to prevent scorching.

3. Store
Store in heavy-duty storage bags or glass jars in the freezer or a cool room with temperatures below 55°F (13°C).

Drying Nuts

Anyone with a nut tree on their property knows there are only so many you can eat. After a while, you can't even give them away! Drying nuts and legumes lets you (and all of your friends) enjoy them all year. Follow specific instructions when drying nuts. Tree nuts (such as almonds, hazelnuts, and walnuts) are dried using different methods than legumes (such as peanuts).

What You'll Need

Nuts

Drying screens or burlap sacks

Heavy-duty storage bags or glass jars

For peanuts: Peanuts are a legume and can be dried at higher temperatures than most nuts. You can dry peanuts in or out of their shells.

1. Wash
Wash peanuts well.

2. Dehydrate
Dry peanuts in or out of their shells in a single layer in a dehydrator at 130°F (54°C) until crisp and dry, approximately 10 hours.

3. Store
Store in tightly sealed heavy-duty storage bags or glass jars. For best results, store bags or jars in the freezer or a cool room with temperatures below 55°F (13°C).

Roasting Nuts and Seeds

You can roast dried seeds and nuts in the oven, keeping the temperature between 250°F and 300°F (121°C and 149°C). Roast seeds for about 10 minutes and nuts for up to 40 minutes, stirring often to prevent scorching.

For almonds, hazelnuts, and walnuts: Nuts, such as almonds, hazelnuts, and walnuts, must be dried before eating. Begin drying within 24 hours of harvest. Nuts may be dried shelled or unshelled.

1. Prepare for drying
Spread nuts on a drying screen, or place in burlap sacks.

2. Dry
Dry in a warm, dry room for about 4 days. The temperature in the room should be between 95°F and 100°F (35°C and 38°C) for best results.

3. Store
Once firm and dry, with a "snap" when cut open, store in heavy-duty storage bags or glass jars in the freezer or a cool room with temperatures below 55°F (13°C). Use within 1 year.

Chestnut Caution

Be careful not to eat horse chestnuts, as they are poisonous! Horse chestnuts are covered with a leathery, often spiny fruit capsule containing two or three glossy nuts, and have fanlike, toothed leaves that emerge from the same point in clusters of five to seven. Edible chestnuts have a sharp, bristly husk that contains two or three nuts, with leaves that originate along the stem.

For chestnuts: Chestnuts are more perishable than other types of nuts, as they are high in starch and low in fat. For short-term storage, keep them in the refrigerator.

1. Pack and dry
Spread chestnuts on a drying screen or place in burlap sacks. Dry in a warm, dry room between 95°F and 100°F (35°C and 38°C) for about 4 days.

2. Store
Once rock hard and dry, store in heavy-duty storage bags or glass jars in the freezer or a cool room with temperatures below 55°F (13°C). Use within 1 year.

Part 3

Canning Food Basics

Canning is an easy and economical means of preserving food. I discuss everything you need to know about safe practices for boiling-water canning. Once you've mastered the basics, you'll quickly be on your way to putting up the season's bounty of jams, jellies, tomato products, pickles, and more!

Tools and Equipment for Canning Food

This section details some of the most common pieces of equipment you are likely to need for canning. Be sure to read recipes and instructions carefully to determine the specific equipment you need before you start canning. You don't want to get halfway through a project and realize you've forgotten something!

Essential Equipment

The following are the must-have pieces of equipment for canning.

Boiling-water canner

A boiling-water canner, or water-bath canner, is made of porcelain-covered steel or aluminum. These large pots with tight-fitting lids and jar racks are used to can high-acid foods, such as jams, jellies, pickles, and fruits.

Choosing Your Canner

Canners are available with either ridged or flat bottoms. Be sure to choose the correct canner for your cooking appliance. Flat-bottomed canners must be used when cooking on any electric element, while either flat or ridged canners will work on gas burners. If you have an induction stove or cooktop, check with the manufacturer of both your cooking appliance and your canner before proceeding to be sure you will be able to can safely without damaging your appliance.

Canning jars

Tempered-glass "Mason"-type jars that can be fitted with two-piece lids are the safest choice for home canning. Approved choices for home canning are 4-ounce (118.25-mL), half-pint, pint, and quart jars. Pint and quart jars are available in both regular-mouth and wide-mouth widths.

Size Matters

Choose your jar based on the size and type of food you are canning, as well as the jar size called for in the recipe. For instance, fruits are less likely to float in a standard-mouth jar, as the "shoulders" of the jar hold it in place, while pickles are better suited to a wide-mouth jar, as it's easier to remove larger pieces. And while you will find an array of jar sizes, be aware that not all of them are approved for canning. For instance, 12-ounce (354.75-mL) jelly jars have not been approved for safe use by the USDA, and jars larger than a quart cannot be safely canned. Save these for other projects, such as fresh pickles and crafts.

Reusable Lids?

Reusable lids, such as those made by Tattler, are the talk of the canning world. But are they safe? While many home canners have had success with these lids, and the idea of using something that does not have to be thrown away after a single use appeals to environmentalists and thrifty homekeepers alike, the USDA has not approved reusable lids for safe home canning use. Without further research, the safest bet may be to stick with standard two-piece lids.

Two-piece lids

Canning lids are comprised of a lid, which has a rubber seal that adheres to the jar, and a screw band, which tightens over the lid to hold it in place until a vacuum seal occurs. While screw bands can be reused as long as they are not dented or rusted, you must always use new lids for each canning project. Once jars are processed and cooled, remove the screw bands for storage. Make sure you also choose the appropriate-size lid for your jars.

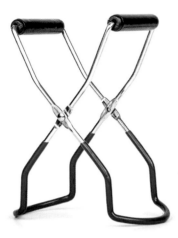

Jar lifter

A jar lifter makes it easy to safely remove hot jars from your canner. These heatproof tongs are designed to gently remove jars by the neck without disturbing the bands or seals. Don't try to substitute regular tongs for this purpose—they will damage your screw bands and greatly increase your chances of dropping extremely hot canned goods all over your kitchen.

Lid wand

A lid wand is a heatproof tool with a small magnet at the end. Use it to safely remove hot lids from simmering water without burning your fingers.

Jar funnel

A jar funnel has a wider mouth than regular kitchen funnels, allowing you to quickly and neatly fill jars with hot foods.

Bubble remover/headspace tool

This inexpensive, multifunction plastic tool removes air pockets from your foods before canning. It also has helpful notches that allow you to check headspace (the amount of space at the top of the jar). Leaving the appropriate amount of headspace is essential for safe and successful canning.

Flea Market Finds

It's easy to find affordable canning jars and pickling crocks at flea markets and garage sales. I've even found "new in box" jars! Jars can be used again and again as long as they're in good condition. Just be sure to check the jars for minute scratches and chips. Discard the jars that do, as they can harbor bacteria or break during processing, and are not safe for canning. Check stoneware pickling crocks before use to be sure there are no cracks or chips on the interior, too. If you shop for flea market stoneware finds, you'll also want to make sure the crocks are glazed on the inside as well as the outside and don't contain harmful substances, such as lead or cadmium. In the end, new crocks are the safest choice.

Jelly bag

A jelly bag is a very fine strainer used to strain juice for jelly making. While you can improvise a jelly bag with a fine-mesh strainer lined with several layers of cheesecloth, there is no substitute for a jelly bag if you want clear, sparkling, perfect jellies.

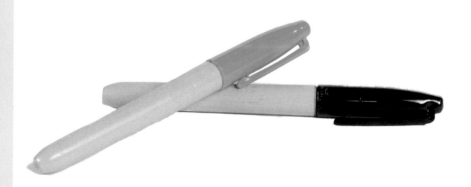

Permanent markers

Label food containers or paper to place on the containers with permanent markers. Rather than use labels, I like to label my canned goods right on the lid; that way, I don't have to scrub labels from jars, and I know at a glance that the lid has been used.

Candy thermometer

Some jam and jelly recipes require the use of a candy thermometer to ensure the food has cooked to a temperature that will allow it to gel. Look for an easy-to-read thermometer that clips securely to the side of your pot without touching the bottom, and read all the instructions for it before use.

Kitchen towels/paper towels

Have plenty of clean, lint-free kitchen towels on hand. You will find countless uses for them, such as jar wiping, cleaning, drying blanched fruits and veggies, and lining your kitchen counter to cool jars.

Timer

Timing is of vital importance for safe canning. If you're purchasing a timer, choose one that can be set for longer periods of time, such as 80+ minutes. You may want to have more than one if you're timing multiple projects. You can even find a portable timer that clips to your apron or hangs around your neck!

The Extras

While you can certainly complete most canning projects without the following tools, each of them makes the work easier. You may even find you have some or all of these in your kitchen already.

Kitchen scale

Many canning products specify foods by weight, as it would be difficult (and downright silly) to measure 22 pounds (10 kg) tomatoes in cups. Adding a manual or digital scale to your kitchen equipment will make things much easier when you have to handle large quantities of food.

Food mill

A food mill purées food while separating the skins and seeds. It is an indispensable tool for making tomato sauce and fruit purées. A manual food mill rests on the side of your bowl or pot and is cranked by hand. Those who prepare many bushels of tomatoes each summer might consider investing in a mechanized food mill.

Food processor

A food processor is a multipurpose tool that can help you slice cabbage for sauerkraut, chop peppers and onions for salsa, or make quick fruit purées (just remove the skins and seeds first).

Cherry pitter

If you're going to be canning cherries, you'll want to invest in this handy, inexpensive tool. It pits olives, too!

Apple corer or slicer

You can use a simple apple corer to remove cores, as long as you don't mind peeling with a paring knife. If you process lots of apples at a time, you might want a hand-cranked tool that peels, cores, and slices all at once.

Other Basic Kitchen Utensils

In addition to the essential canning equipment listed previously, you'll want to have the following basic kitchen equipment on hand:

- Sharp, well-maintained kitchen knives (including a chef's knife and a paring knife)
- Cutting board
- Cookware: heavy, nonreactive, stainless-steel stock pots and saucepans (no aluminum, tin, copper, or cast-iron cookware)
- Measuring cups and spoons
- Mixing bowls
- Colander and fine-mesh strainer
- Wooden and nonreactive metal spoons
- Ladle
- Vegetable peeler
- Potato masher
- Heavy-duty potholders
- Chinese strainer or large slotted spoon
- Double boiler
- Steamer insert

Cooling racks

Heavy-duty cooling racks make a great landing spot for hot jars that need to rest undisturbed.

What Is pH?

Whether a food is acid or alkaline is determined by its pH (per-Hydrogen) level, a measurement of hydrogen ion concentration. In chemistry, 7.0 is considered a neutral pH level. For the purpose of home canning, the cutoff point between acid (low-pH) foods and alkaline (high-pH) foods is 4.6. Botulism cannot survive in an acid environment with a pH below 4.6.

Part 3: Canning Food Basics

The Science Behind Canning

Fresh foods have a high water content and contain enzymes, bacteria, molds, and yeasts that contribute to spoilage. Food spoils as water is lost, microorganisms grow, and enzymatic processes break down the cell walls. Exposure to oxygen (*oxidation*) also contributes to food spoilage.

Canning at appropriate temperatures using the correct method for the correct length of time eliminates or greatly reduces these factors, allowing food to be stored for much longer periods of time. Oxygen is removed, allowing liquids and solids to remain stable. Enzymes are destroyed, slowing cellular deterioration. Bacteria, yeasts, and molds are eliminated through high-temperature processing and, sometimes, acidification of foods. A proper vacuum seal keeps liquid in the jar and air and microorganisms out.

Acidity

Safe processing temperatures are determined by the acidity of the food. High-acid foods with a pH below 4.6 can be safely canned in a boiling-water canner, which heats foods to 212°F (100°C), a temperature sufficient to destroy spoilers. Low-acid foods with a pH above 4.6 require higher temperatures to destroy these same spoilers and must be processed in a pressure canner in order to heat the jars to 240°F (116°C).

Time

Time is of the essence. Foods must be heated for a specific period of time in order for every molecule to reach the appropriate temperature. *Viscosity,* which describes the density, thickness, and molecular makeup of a particular food, is another important factor in this process. Extremely viscous foods made from fibrous vegetables, such as pumpkin and squash purées or butters, are not approved for home canning because the viscosity of the product does not allow each molecule to be heated to the appropriate temperature.

The canning process seems daunting, but it's really simple. Food is packed in jars using tested, approved methods. Lids are then affixed and held in place with a screw band. As the heat of the water increases, the food expands, and air is forced out of the jar. As this occurs, the lid is affixed to the jar, creating a vacuum seal. The action of convection moves the liquid around in the jar, ensuring even heating. As this occurs, high temperatures destroy spoilers, such as enzymes, bacteria, molds, and yeasts.

Think of canned foods as being in a state of "suspended animation." Once opened, treat them the same way you would fresh foods. An open jar is once again susceptible to spoilage and should be refrigerated after opening and consumed within about 1 week.

Altitude

The final factor that must be considered when canning is altitude. As altitude increases, water boils at a lower temperature. For this reason, foods must be processed for longer periods of time. You can find altitude adjustment charts and detailed information in "Processing Times"; read this material thoroughly if you are located more than 1,001 feet (305 m) above sea level.

Food Safety and Safe Food Handling

Food safety is no joke. Improperly canned foods can cause foodborne illnesses, with consequences that range from a bad tummy ache to, in the worst cases, death. Proper sanitation practices and an understanding of the science of home canning principles are essential. Read this section thoroughly and follow all the instructions to ensure your home-canned foods are both safe and delicious.

Canning and Bacteria

Canning allows you to create shelf-stable foods that can be stored for much longer periods of time than fresh foods. This is achieved by heating food in jars for a precise period of time to a temperature that eliminates spoilers and forces air out of the jars, creating a vacuum seal.

Canning creates an anaerobic (oxygen-free) environment, so it is important to follow instructions carefully to avoid the most dangerous type of foodborne illness: botulism.

What Is Botulism?

The most dangerous of all bacterial spoilers is botulism, which is caused by the growth of the bacterium *Clostridium botulinum*. These spores are present in water and soil and can remain dormant and harmless for long periods of time. However, under ideal conditions—such as a moist, low-acid medium; temperatures between 40°F and 120°F (4°C and 49°C); and the absence of oxygen (an *anaerobic* environment)—these harmless spores can quickly develop into vegetative cells that multiply rapidly, producing deadly levels of toxin in as little as 3 days.

If eaten, even very small amounts of this toxin can produce serious illness. Improperly processed home-canned vegetables are among the foods most commonly contaminated, along with home-cured meats and fish, honey, and corn syrup.

Symptoms of botulism poisoning appear within 8 to 24 hours of consuming contaminated foods, and include blurred or double vision, abdominal cramps, difficulty swallowing or speaking, nausea, vomiting, paralysis or extreme muscle weakness occurring on both sides of the body, and breathing difficulty (which can lead to respiratory failure). If you exhibit any of these symptoms, seek medical attention immediately.

Infant botulism occurs when an infant eats food that contains spores, which then grow in the gastrointestinal tract. Never feed honey, corn syrup, or home-canned vegetables to children under 2 years of age.

Botulism infection is rare, but it must be taken seriously. Observe proper sanitation methods, pressure can low-acid foods using the appropriate methods, and never consume suspect foods. Immediate medical attention greatly reduces the chances of death.

To prevent botulism, can foods using appropriate methods, and examine all canned goods before eating (see "Identifying and Disposing of Spoiled Food" for more information). Never eat food from a jar that is bulging, smells "off," or has bubbling or spurting liquid. Home-canned vegetables should be cooked at a boil for 10 minutes before eating.

Kitchen Sanitation

In addition to *C. botulinum,* safe canning practices also greatly reduce the risk of contamination from bacteria, such as *listeria, salmonella, Campylobacter,* and *E. coli,* which can all cause unpleasant—and even deadly—foodborne illnesses.

Cleaning and sanitizing your kitchen and work tools is the essential first step in home canning safety. Clean all hard surfaces with a sanitizing solution of 1 teaspoon chlorine bleach to 1 quart water. When using the solution, pay careful attention to sinks, counters, and cutting boards, but remember to wipe down all surfaces you'll be touching, including doorknobs and refrigerator handles.

Canning jars should be washed and sterilized before use. If your dishwasher has a "sanitize" cycle that reaches 160°F (71°C), you can sterilize jars during the wash cycle. Otherwise, wash jars in plenty of hot, soapy water, and then heat them in a boiling-water canner with water to cover them by 2 inches (5 cm). Set a timer for 10 minutes once the water reaches a boil, and then turn heat to low and keep hot until ready to use. It is not necessary to sterilize jars if foods will be pressure canned or processed in a boiling-water canner for more than 10 minutes.

Ensure all the tools you will be using are clean, too. Wash knives, spoons, saucepans, canning tools, and any other items that will touch your food in hot, soapy water. Dirty kitchen towels are also a source of contaminants, so have a supply of clean, freshly washed towels on hand for each project.

Proper hand washing is your final line of defense against foodborne illnesses. Wash your hands with hot, soapy water (it's not necessary to use antibacterial soap) before and after each task—washing vegetables, getting things in and out of the refrigerator, answering the phone, or filling jars. Wash all surfaces of your hands, paying particular attention to your fingernails, for as long as it takes to recite the alphabet or sing the "Happy Birthday" song to yourself (note: you don't need to sing it aloud!). You really can't wash your hands too often.

Make sure you also wash and rinse foods that are to be canned in plenty of running water. In addition to bacteria, yeasts, and molds, vegetables can also harbor insects and their eggs. Root vegetables, such as carrots or parsnips, should be washed before and after peeling for safest handling. Do not can overripe foods, those from frost-killed vines, or foods showing significant signs of spoilage, such as soft spots and bruising.

Follow the Rules

Boiling-water and pressure canning are the only safe, approved methods for home canning of foods. Unsafe methods include open-kettle canning (in which food is cooked in an ordinary kettle, and then packed without processing); dishwasher, oven, or microwave canning; canning in a pressure cooker; and steam canning. None of these methods can be guaranteed to heat foods uniformly and to the appropriate temperature to eliminate dangerous spoilers. Canning powders, which purport to preserve foods through the addition of aspirin (salicylic acid) rather than heat processing, should also be avoided at all costs.

A proper vacuum seal is essential for safety, so two-piece lids—consisting of a sealable lid and screw band—should be used to can foods. Avoid jars with wire bails and glass caps, one-piece lids, paraffin wax, and glass or zinc caps with rubber rings.

Follow approved, updated methods for home canning. Scientific discoveries have greatly improved the safety of home canning, so what may have been deemed safe in your grandmother's day might not apply today. For your family's safety, you should also use updated, tested recipes. Generally, if your source is more than 4 years old, look to more recent sources before proceeding.

Above all, don't improvise. Cooking is an art, but canning is a science, and there are many factors that affect foods safety (such as acidity, temperature, and viscosity). Take safety seriously in your kitchen!

Foods Recommended for Boiling-Water Canning

As you've learned, food acidity determines which processing method you have to use. Acid foods with a pH below 4.6 can be safely canned in a boiling-water canner.

Foods can be considered low pH or acid for several reasons. They may be naturally acidic, such as most fruits. They may also be acidified through fermentation or the addition of lemon juice, vinegar, or citric acid.

Acid foods include the following:

- Fruit with or without sugar syrup, such as apples, berries, cranberries, peaches, and pears
- Sugar jams, jellies, and preserves
- Pickled fruits and vegetables
- Tomato products, such as salsa, canned tomatoes, and ketchup, that have been acidified with bottled lemon juice or citric acid
- Relishes and chutneys

Foods Recommended for Pressure Canning

Since botulism spores can survive in a low-acid (alkaline) environment, certain foods must be heated to higher temperatures in order to eliminate all spoilers. It is essential to can these foods with low acidity (pH above 4.6) in a pressure canner. (See Part 8, "Pressure Canning," for detailed instructions on pressure canning.)

Alkaline foods include the following:

- Vegetables
- Soups and stocks
- Meat, poultry, and fish
- Mixtures of acid and alkaline foods, such as stewed tomatoes and certain tomato sauces and salsas
- Borderline fruits that have not been acidified, such as tomatoes, figs, Asian pears, melons, bananas, dates, persimmons, and ripe pineapples

Borderline Foods

Some fruits have a borderline acidity level and should be treated with extra care. For instance, figs should always be canned using approved recipes that follow current USDA safety guidelines.

Tomatoes used to be considered a high-acid food, but in recent years, sweeter varieties have led food scientists to consider tomatoes a borderline food, with an acidity that hovers just above or below a pH of 4.6. For this reason, tomato products should be canned in a boiling-water canner only if they have been sufficiently acidified. Some tomato products, such as stewed tomatoes, must always be canned in a pressure canner, as the addition of alkaline vegetables lowers the overall acidity of the food. If you prefer not to acidify your tomatoes, follow the instructions provided in Part 8, "Pressure Canning," for pressure canning tomatoes.

Preparing the Jars and Equipment

Once you've familiarized yourself with the basics, gathered your equipment, sterilized your kitchen, and picked or shopped for fresh produce, you're ready to get started! You can now follow these easy steps to prepare your jars and equipment.

Mason Jars

Mason jars—named for their inventor, John Landis Mason—may be reused many times; you only need to add a new lid for each use. While standard lids fit many commercial jars, such as mayonnaise-type jars, these are not recommended for home canning, as they are not tempered for the same level of heat resistance. Use glass jars intended for canning to avoid seal failure and breakage.

1. Examine canner and jars

Ensure your boiling-water canner has a rack and lid that fit securely. Look for scratches or chips in jars, as bacteria can hide in these crevices. Recycle any damaged jars.

2. Examine lids

Use new lids every time, and check the rubber seals to be sure they are not cracked or brittle. Discard lids that are dented, misshapen, or have gaps in the rubber seal.

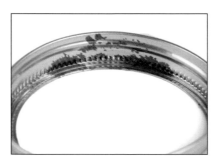

3. Examine screw bands

Be sure they are not dented or misshapen, as this will prevent a proper vacuum seal. Discard any damaged or rusted bands.

4. Wash jars and equipment

Wash all jars and equipment you will be using in hot, soapy water, and allow them to air dry. You can also wash jars in the dishwasher, but make sure to rinse well.

5. Preheat the canner

Center the canner on the burner, and place the jar rack in the canner. Fill halfway with warm water. Begin to heat the water over medium-low heat as you prepare the remaining equipment.

6. Preheat jars

If you aren't sterilizing your jars, submerge them right side up in the canner to preheat them. Keep jars submerged in simmering water until you're ready to fill them.

7. Heat a kettle or pot of water

Once you're ready to process your jars, you'll need to add hot water to cover the jars by 2 inches (5 cm). Heat a large kettle of water over medium heat, so you'll have hot water at the ready.

8. Simmer lids

Place lids in a small saucepan with warm water, and bring to a simmer over low heat just before you begin to fill the jars with food.

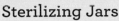

Sterilizing Jars

Jars must be sterilized if food is to be processed for less than 10 minutes in a boiling-water canner. Immerse jars right side up in a boiling-water canner with water to cover them by 1 inch (2.5 cm), and put the lids on. Bring to a boil over high heat; when the water boils (you'll see steam escaping), set a kitchen timer for 10 minutes. After 10 minutes, turn heat to low to keep jars warm, and proceed with your recipe.

Preparing the Food

Clean kitchen, clean hands, and clean equipment—you're now ready to start canning! Read on to learn how to prepare food for boiling-water canning.

1. Select produce

Aim for "vine to brine" in 24 hours or less for best results!

The best food for successful home canning is farm or field fresh, perfectly ripe produce. Choose unblemished foods at the peak of their season.

2. Prepare ingredients

Read through the recipe, and gather all the ingredients and equipment you will need before you begin.

3. Wash produce

Wash produce well in plenty of cool, running water. It's important to eliminate dirt, insects and their eggs, and other contaminants before canning.

4a. Blanch produce

Most fruits and vegetables will benefit from blanching, which is a dip in boiling water followed by rapid cooling to loosen skins and deactivate enzymes that lead to deterioration.

4b. Pretreat produce

Refer to Parts 3 through 7 for recommended pretreatment options for particular foods.

Use a commercial preparation, such as Fruit-Fresh, or use a solution of citric acid or lemon juice.

Hot or Raw Pack?

There are two types of pack used in canning: *hot pack,* in which the food has been heated to a boil in a liquid medium before it is packed in jars, or *raw pack,* in which food is packed raw into jars and covered with the boiling canning medium. In most cases, the hot-pack method produces more desirable results.

5. Choose the correct pack

Select the right type of pack for the food you are canning. While most fruits and vegetables benefit from a hot pack, more delicate items like peas and berries are better when packed raw.

6. Choose the correct canning medium

Fruits may be packed in water, juice, or simple syrup, while tomatoes may be packed in water or homemade tomato juice. Refer to each part for specific recommendations for each type of food.

7. Prepare food

Follow the recipes and instructions carefully to ensure a safe product with desirable texture, color, and flavor.

Processing the Food and Jars

It's now time to fill your hot, clean jars with freshly harvested, carefully prepared food. You're nearly there! Choose a recipe for a jam, jelly, tomato product, or pickle that appeals to you and your family. Read the recipe several times before you begin your first canning project.

1. Fill jars

Carefully remove hot jars from the canner with a jar lifter, and use a jar funnel and ladle to fill jars with hot food.

2. Remove bubbles

Use a bubbling tool or a plastic butter knife to gently remove air pockets and bubbles from the food.

3. Check and adjust headspace

Leave the correct amount of space at the top of your jar to create a proper seal. Use the notched end of your jar bubbler to check headspace and adjust headspace after bubbling.

4. Wipe jar rims

Use hot water and a clean paper towel or kitchen towel to wipe the rim of each jar to make sure they are perfectly clean.

Bubble, Bubble, Toil and Trouble

Removing excess air from foods to be canned, also known as *bubbling,* is an essential step. Air pockets can harbor spoilers and can also affect the *headspace,* or the amount of space left at the top of the jar. Therefore, make sure you use a jar bubbler every single time. Use plastic utensils only, as metal utensils can create minute scratches inside your canning jars, leading to damage or spoilage.

5. Affix lids

Use a magnetic lid lifter to fish lids out of the simmering water. Affix lids on clean jar rims, and tighten screw bands to fingertip tightness.

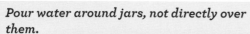

Pour water around jars, not directly over them.

6. Submerge jars and cover

Raise the rack to suspend it inside the canner, and place jars on the rack. Using oven mitts, submerge the rack, and add hot water to cover jars by 1 to 2 inches (2.5 to 5 cm).

7. Cover canner and set timer

Cover the canner, and bring to a boil over high heat. When steam escapes from around the lid and the water is at a rolling boil, set a timer for the processing time recommended in the recipe.

Fingertip Tightness

Screw bands should be tightened to "fingertip tightness." What does that mean? Too tight, and you'll trap air in the jar; too loose, and your jars will leak and fail to seal. The release of air is essential to create a vacuum seal, so screw the bands on with your fingertips just until you meet a little resistance.

8. Turn off heat and remove lid

When the processing time is over, remove the canner lid and let jars rest undisturbed for 5 minutes.

9. Remove jars

Use a jar lifter to carefully remove jars from the canner, keeping them upright. Place jars on a folded towel or cooling rack, and allow to cool undisturbed for 12 to 24 hours.

Monitoring Water Levels

During longer processing times and when processing quart jars, you may need to add more water to the canner. Monitor water levels by taking a quick peek under the lid of the canner. If the water level has dropped below the recommended 1 to 2 inches (2.5 to 5 cm) above the jar lids, add more boiling water.

10. Remove screw bands and check seals

Remove screw bands, and test seals by pressing the center of each lid. If you are able to indent the lid, the seal has failed. Lift each jar by its edges.

11. Wash, label, and store jars

Wash sealed jars in warm water with a little soap. Label lids with the food, date processed, and batch number. Store in a cool, dark, dry location for up to 1 year.

Boiling-Water Canning Processing Times

Canned food will spoil if you fail to follow the correct processing times. To destroy microorganisms, jars must be processed for the correct amount of time and cooled at room temperature. Several factors can affect processing times, including the pH of the food you are canning, viscosity, pack method, and altitude.

Always use a tested recipe when canning, which specifies processing times. For your convenience, refer to the following table for processing times for foods commonly processed in a water bath. While overprocessing is generally not harmful from a safety perspective, it will degrade the quality of the foods you are canning. Stick to the recommended times for best results.

If you live at an elevation of more than 1,000 feet (306 m) above sea level, water boils at a lower temperature. For instance, if you are 1,200 feet (366 m) above sea level, your water will boil at 210°F (99°C), rather than 212°F (100°C). This lower boiling point provides an insufficient amount of heat to eliminate spoilers. In order to safely process foods, it is essential to increase the processing time for all boiling-water canning recipes. Use the following chart as a guideline, and contact your county extension agent or local government service organization for more information.

Altitude in Feet (Meters)	Increase Processing Time By
1,001 to 3,000 (305 to 914)	5 minutes
3,001 to 6,000 (915 to 1,828)	10 minutes
6,001 to 8,000 (1,829 to 2,438)	15 minutes
8,001 to 10,000 (2,439 to 3,048)	20 minutes

Food	Pack	Processing Time (in Minutes for Altitudes up to 2,000 Feet [610 m])
Apple butter	Hot	Half-pint or pint: 10
Apples	Hot	Pint or quart: 25
Berries	Hot	Pint or quart: 20
	Raw	Pint: 20
		Quart: 25
Cherries	Hot	Pint: 20
		Quart: 25
	Raw	Pint or quart: 30
Fruit purée	Hot	Pint or quart: 20
Grape juice	Hot	Pint or quart: 10
Peaches and apricots, halves or slices	Hot	Pint: 25
		Quart: 30
	Raw	Pint: 35
		Quart: 40
Pears, halves or slices	Hot	Pint: 25
		Quart: 30
Plums, halved or whole	Hot or raw	Pint: 25
		Quart: 30
Pickles, dill	Raw	Pint: 15
		Quart: 20
Sauerkraut	Raw	Pint: 25
		Quart: 30
Tomatoes, whole	Raw, no added liquid	Pint or quart: 90

Troubleshooting the Canning Process

Things can and will go wrong in the kitchen, and it's best to be prepared. It's important to be able to identify spoiled food versus food that is less than appealing to the eye. Be prepared, and always reprocess foods according to outlined methods. As always, your motto should be, "When in doubt, throw it out!"

Basic Safety Precautions

In addition to obvious signs of spoilage, it is important to be vigilant about botulism, which is sometimes undetectable. Keep an eye out for leakage, spurting liquid, or foods that bubble in the jar. Always be certain that your pressure canner is in good working order, and that you have followed all recommendations for sanitation, food selection, and processing exactly.

Always follow these safety precautions when consuming canned low-acid foods:

- Never taste food before heating it.
- Bring canned foods to a boil in a saucepan, and boil for 10 minutes, or reduce heat and simmer for 15 minutes.
- Do not heat pressure-canned foods in a microwave. The uneven heat can leave cold spots.
- If preparing casseroles or baked dishes from canned goods, cook until the temperature of the food reaches 185°F (85°C) on an instant-read thermometer.

Power Failure

If electricity or gas is lost during boiling-water canning, take the following measures:

- If power is restored quickly and the jars are still warm, reprocess the jars for the entire time specified in the recipe.
- If it's not possible to reprocess the jars immediately, store them at 40°F (4°C) up to overnight. Replace the lids with new, unused lids, and reprocess for the entire time specified in the recipe.
- If power or gas will be out for several days, try to reprocess the jars at another location, remove food from jars and freeze instead, or cook and consume immediately.

Jars Did Not Seal

Canned foods can be reprocessed if the jar did not seal during processing. Generally, this step is worthwhile only if an entire batch fails to seal. If a single jar does not seal, freeze the contents, or cook and eat immediately.

To reprocess jars, determine the reason for failure. If an entire batch fails to seal, it's most likely that the seals on the lids were old or faulty. Remove the lid and inspect the sealing rim of the jar. If the jar itself is not defective, readjust the headspace, wipe the sealing edge, and affix a *new* two-piece lid (remember to simmer the lids first to soften the seal). If just a few seals have failed, you may not need new screw bands. Inspect them to be sure they are *true* (perfectly round), and replace if necessary. Reprocess the jars for the entire amount of time recommended in the recipe.

Loss of Liquid in Jars

Loss of liquid in jars, or *siphoning,* is not in itself an indication of spoilage. Liquid loss can occur for any of the following reasons. If no other signs of spoilage are present, it is safe to consume.

- **Air bubbles and pockets in jar:** Remove all air pockets with a bubble remover before processing.
- **Food packed too tightly, or improper headspace:** Follow instructions to the letter, and measure headspace before sealing jars.
- **Poor seal:** Use new lids every time, and tighten bands to fingertip tightness—not too loose, not too tight.

Cloudy Liquid in Jars

Cloudy liquid is not a sign of spoilage on its own. If no other signs of spoilage are present, it is generally safe to eat. For future canning efforts, consider the following:

- **Minerals in water:** If you have hard water, choose distilled or softened water for canning.
- **Additives in salt:** Choose additive-free salt, such as canning, pickling, or kosher salt.

Floating Fruit

Floating fruit is usually not a sign of spoilage on its own. All fruit contains air in its cells. Some fruits, such as berries, apricots, and peaches, have more air in their cells and are more likely to float. Raw-packed tomatoes are also likely to float. (See Part 6, "Canning Tomatoes and Tomato Products," for more detailed information on tomato canning.) Consider the following ways of avoiding this:

- **Use hot pack rather than raw.** Raw packed fruits shrink when heated during the canning process, increasing the likelihood of floating.

- **Change the syrup type.** Use a heavy syrup for fruits that are likely to float.

- **Don't use overripe fruit.** Overripe fruit is more likely to float due to cellular breakdown.

- **Do not overprocess.** This will also contribute to cellular breakdown.

When in Doubt, Throw It Out!

Never eat food from a jar that does not "pop" when you open it, as this is a sign that the seal has failed. Do not eat food from jars with bulging lids, spurting liquids, or an "off" odor.

Food Is Dark or Discolored (but Not Spoiled)

Food may darken due to underprocessing, siphoning of liquid during the canning process, failing to properly pretreat, or raw packing foods that should be hot packed (such as pears). Some fruits will also turn pink during dry, hot weather.

Discolored food is generally safe to eat if the liquid is clear, no "off" odor is present, and you have observed the recommended processing time, temperature, and method. Again, follow all instructions, check the seals carefully, and use recommended methods—there are no shortcuts in home canning.

Jar Seals and Then Unseals

The food is spoiled. See "Identifying and Disposing of Spoiled Food" for safe handling and disposal instructions.

Identifying and Disposing of Spoiled Food

Being able to identify spoiled food and dispose of it safely is of crucial importance. Read the following guidelines carefully!

Examine Food Before Eating

Store jars in a cool, dark place, without their screw bands. It is much easier to identify spoiled food in a jar stored without its band because the telltale spoilage sign of a leaky jar will be immediately obvious to the eye. To examine canned foods for spoilage, follow these steps:

1. Press the seal at the top of the jar. If it is properly sealed, it won't move. If you can move the seal, or if the lid has swelled or loosened, the food is spoiled.

2. Hold the jar upright at eye level in a well-lit area. Look for streaks of food that have escaped from the jar after storage and any bubbling inside the jar. If either of these signs is present, the food is spoiled.

3. Open the jar and look for spurting or bubbling liquid. Examine for cottonlike mold growth that can be blue, white, black, or green on the food and the underside of the lid. If any of these signs is present, the food is spoiled.

Never taste foods to see if they are spoiled—when in doubt, throw it out.

Use Safe Disposal Practices

It is of vital importance to dispose of spoiled foods in a way that will not expose humans or animals to their contents.

If jars are still sealed, place them in a heavy garbage bag and tape it shut. Seal this inside another garbage bag, and dispose of it as you would regular trash.

If jars are unsealed or leaking, they must be detoxified using the following process. Wear heavy disposable gloves during this process; botulism is toxic whether ingested or absorbed through the skin, so never handle suspect foods without gloves.

1. Carefully place the suspect jars (with contents intact) on their sides in an 8-quart or larger stock pot or boiling-water canner.

2. Wash your hands with the gloves still on, being very careful not to splash water.

3. Carefully add water to the pot to cover the jars by more than 1 inch (2.5 cm).

4. Bring to a boil. Boil jars for 30 minutes to destroy any toxins present in food.

5. Cool completely. Dispose of food and containers in a sealed trash bag.

! *Wear gloves throughout this process to avoid contact with skin.*

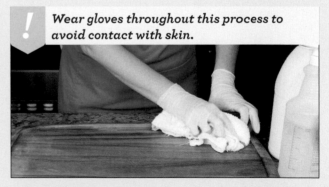

6. Spray all kitchen surfaces with a solution of 1 cup chlorine bleach to 5 cups water. Let stand for 30 minutes, and then wipe with paper towels. Dispose of paper towels in a sealed trash bag. Repeat, and wash all surfaces with soap and hot water.

Identifying and Disposing of Spoiled Food

Part 4

Canning Fruits and Pie Fillings

Canning captures the flavor of delicious, seasonal fruits. You'll love having an array of stone fruits, berries, autumn fruits, and pie fillings in the pantry. And buying fresh fruit in season from local growers saves you money, too!

Canning Whole and Sliced Fruits

When gathering fruit to can, choose firm, perfectly ripe fruit at the peak of its season. Press a piece of fruit; if your fingerprint remains, it's too ripe. You can also use the "sniff test"; a pear should smell like a pear, and give gently to pressure. Underripe fruit contains enzymes that produce undesirable results. Supermarket fruit is usually a poor choice for canning, as it has been picked before ripening and allowed to mature under unnatural conditions.

Most fruits benefit from the hot-pack method, which results in better quality while minimizing issues, such as floating fruit. Hot packing removes air and shrinks tissue before the food is canned, which allows a better "pack" in the jar. Some fruits, such as raspberries, should always be raw packed. The recipes in this part give you specific guidance based on the type of fruit.

The fruits in this part should be processed in a boiling-water canner. The increased boiling point created in a pressure canner will break down the cellular structure of most fruits, resulting in poor quality and flavor.

Most of the recipes in this part and elsewhere in the book are written to make 9 pints or 7 quarts, which is the standard full load of a boiling-water canner. You can halve a recipe if you prefer a smaller batch, but don't double it. Food should be processed immediately after cooking to ensure excellent quality and consistent results.

When a recipe calls for pints or quarts only, do not deviate from this directive. It's particularly important not to can recipes that have been developed and tested for pints only using quart jars, as this can affect heat penetration, rendering an unsafe product.

If you have a choice between pints and quarts, consider your family's eating habits. Will you be able to use a quart-sized jar of peaches or pears before they spoil? Or are pints a better choice for smaller families or smaller appetites? It's all dependent on what you need.

Hot Pack vs. Raw Pack

Very few fruits benefit from a raw pack. Hot packing fruit helps to shrink the cellular structure of the fruit, softening it and making it easier to pack in jars. Soft berries, such as raspberries, blackberries, and blueberries, hold their shape better when raw-packed. Strawberries do not can well; they break down and lose their color regardless of the pack or canning medium. Firmer berries, such as cranberries, should either have their skins checked or be hot packed. When in doubt, hot pack fruits for ease of canning and appearance of the finished product. Hot-packed fruit tastes better and is less likely to float in the jars.

Waste Not, Want Not

After you enjoy your canned fruit, you'll have some syrup left over in the jar. The syrup will take on some of the flavors of the fruit, so it makes a great ingredient. Before you throw it away, consider the following uses:

- **Pancake syrup:** Add a little vanilla or maple extract and reduce the syrup in a small saucepan until thick.

- **Recipes:** Replace some or all of the syrup in a recipe with canning syrup (bread pudding is a perfect example). Be sure to reduce the overall liquid in your recipe.

- **Beverages:** Pour a little canning syrup into a tall glass with plenty of ice, and then top with soda water for a refreshing fruit soda. Or use canning liquid as the base for a delicious cocktail or to sweeten your hot or iced tea.

- **Baking:** Try pouring warm syrup over a freshly baked cake while it's still warm.

Choosing and Making Canning Liquids

Fruits can be canned in a variety of liquids. When choosing a canning medium, consider the intended use of your canned fruit. Here are the three main types of canning liquids:

- **Sweetened liquids:** If you will be eating fruit without cooking it further, a sweetened medium, such as simple syrup, is a good choice.
- **Boiling water:** If you'll be using the canned fruit in baked goods, such as cobblers or crisps, boiling water may be a better choice, as you'll be sweetening the fruit before you bake it.
- **Fruit juices:** If you're concerned about adding too much sugar but don't like the flavor of water-canned fruit, unsweetened fruit juices—such as pineapple, apple, or white grape juice—work well.

Sugar does not help to preserve fruit, but it improves its shape, flavor, color, and texture. Sugar adds calories, so experiment and choose the lightest syrup that appeals to you and is sufficient for your needs. You can replace up to half of the sugar in simple syrup with other sweeteners, such as honey, agave nectar, or light corn syrup.

Whether you choose water, fruit juice, or syrup, your canning medium must always be brought to a boil before raw packing in hot jars. When hot packing, boil the fruit in your chosen canning medium for 5 minutes, and then pack in hot jars.

Making Simple Syrup

To make simple syrup for canning, refer to the following chart to choose the correct syrup weight. Add sugar and water to a heavy saucepan, and stir over medium heat until syrup is boiling and sugar has completely dissolved. Use immediately.

Making Simple Syrup

Syrup Type	Approximate Percentage of Sugar	Sugar (in Cups)	Water (in Cups)	Uses
Light	20	For 9 pints: 1½	For 9 pints: 5¾	Use light syrup for very sweet fruits, or when you don't want to add too much sugar. This may not be sweet enough for some tastes.
		For 7 quarts: 2¼	For 7 quarts: 9	
Medium	30	For 9 pints: 2¼	For 9 pints: 5¼	Most fruits can be canned using a medium syrup. For best results, use this for apples, cherries, berries, and grapes.
		For 7 quarts: 3¾	For 7 quarts: 8¼	
Heavy	40	For 9 pints: 3¼	For 9 pints: 5	Use this for tart apples, sour fruits, pears, and most stone fruits* (peaches, nectarines, apricots, and plums).
		For 7 quarts: 5¼	For 7 quarts: 7¾	

While nearly any fruit can be canned using medium syrup, stone fruits, such as peaches, nectarines, and apricots, have a tendency to float. Heavy syrup minimizes this effect.

Canning with Artificial Sweeteners

It is possible to can with artificial sweeteners, but beware. Saccharin and aspartame affect flavor and can result in a bitter finished product. Heat applied during canning can cause artificial sweeteners to lose their "sweet" flavor. For best results, can fruit in plain boiling water and add artificial sweeteners to taste just before serving.

If you do choose to can with artificial sweeteners, the National Center for Home Food Preservation recommends sucralose (Splenda). For every 5½ cups of water, use 1¼ cups sucralose. The results will be similar to canning in water, but with a sweet taste. You can always add more to taste once you're ready to eat the fruit.

Preparing Fruits for Canning

What You'll Need

Canning medium (simple syrup, fruit juice, or boiling water; see "Choosing and Making Canning Liquids")

Treatment solution

Jars

Lids and screw bands

Canner

Fruit

Paring knife

Pot or blancher

Ice bath (depending on fruit)

Potato peeler

Baking pan

Jar funnel

Ladle

Bubble remover

Kitchen towels

Before You Begin

1. Prepare canning medium
Prepare light, medium, or heavy syrup, water, or fruit juice according to the canning medium that is best for your fruit (see "Choosing and Making Canning Liquids").

2. Prepare treatment solution
If you are canning a fruit that is prone to browning, prepare a treatment solution. Use a commercial product, such as Fruit-Fresh, or add 1 crushed 500 mg vitamin C tablet or $1/4$ cup bottled lemon juice to 1 gallon (3.75 L) water.

3. Prepare jars, lids, and canner
Prepare your jars, lids, and canner as outlined in "Preparing the Jars and Equipment." Keep jars and lids on simmer until ready to use.

1. Wash
Wash fruit in plenty of cold, running water.

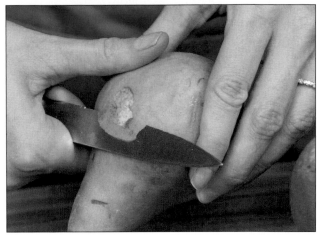

2. Trim
Check the fruit for soft spots or blemishes, and trim them away. Reserve very soft or overripe fruit for immediate consumption.

3. Blanch if necessary
See "Processing Times for Fruits" for detailed instructions for each fruit.

Blanch fruit with peels before peeling by dipping a few pieces at a time into boiling water for just a few seconds to loosen the skins, and then transfer to an ice bath. Treat if necessary.

4. Peel and slice
Peel unblanched fruit with a potato peeler, as you would a potato. Slice all peeled fruit as desired, removing pits and seeds.

5. Heat
If you are hot packing fruit, bring it to a boil in the canning medium, and boil for 5 minutes.

6. Fill jars
Hot pack: Working with one jar at a time, fill each jar with fruit and canning liquid using a jar funnel and ladle if necessary, leaving a headspace of ½ inch (1.25 cm).

Raw pack: Working with one hot jar at a time, pack fruit loosely into the jar, and add boiling canning liquid, leaving ½ inch (1.25 cm) headspace.

7. Remove bubbles and check headspace
Run a bubble remover around the edges of fruit, gently pressing inward so no pockets of air remain. Using the opposite side of the bubble remover, check headspace on each jar. Add or remove liquid if necessary.

8. Clean jar rims and affix lids

Use a clean kitchen towel and hot water to wipe the edge of each jar, removing every speck of food and syrup. Place a hot lid on each jar, and screw the bands to fingertip tightness.

9. Place jars in canner

Gently submerge filled jars in the simmering water, and place on the canning rack. Put the lid on the pot, and turn heat to the highest setting.

10. Process jars

When water has come to a boil and steam begins to escape, begin timing according to the recipe. After that has ended, turn off the heat, remove the canner lid, and let the jars rest for 5 minutes.

11. Cool and store jars

Remove carefully, and set on a heatproof surface lined with kitchen towels for 24 hours. Check seals carefully, and wipe jars clean or rinse under room-temperature running water. Store for up to 2 years.

Processing Times for Fruits

Always process fruit according to tested recipes, using the pack and processing time recommended. You can use the following chart as a guideline for canning most fruits.

Fruit Processing Times

Product	Pack	Processing Time*	Notes**
Apples, sliced	Hot pack	Pints or quarts: 20 minutes	Treat while slicing to prevent browning.
Apricots and nectarines, halved or sliced	Hot pack	Pints: 20 minutes Quarts: 25 minutes	Leave unpeeled if desired.
Berries, firm (cranberries and gooseberries)	Hot pack	Pints or quarts: 15 minutes	When canning gooseberries, use scissors to snip off the heads and tails.
Berries, soft (blueberries, blackberries, raspberries, boysenberries, and elderberries)	Raw pack	Pints: 15 minutes Quarts: 20 minutes	Wash berries in ice water to firm fruit. Add acid to prevent spoilage.
Cherries, whole (sweet or sour)	Hot pack	Pints: 15 minutes Quarts: 20 minutes	Pit cherries if desired.
Grapefruit or orange segments	Raw pack	Pints: 10 minutes Quarts: 10 minutes	To segment citrus fruits, cut away peel and pith, and then hold the fruit in your palm. Carefully cut between membranes to release individual segments.
Grapes, whole	Raw pack	Pints: 15 minutes Quarts: 20 minutes	Leave 1 inch (2.5 cm) headspace in jars.

Product	Pack	Processing Time*	Notes**
Peaches	Hot pack	Pints: 20 minutes Quarts: 25 minutes	Blanch and peel peaches before canning. Treat to prevent browning.
Pears	Hot pack	Pints: 20 minutes Quarts: 25 minutes	Dip in boiling water to loosen skins, and then submerge in an ice bath. Treat to prevent browning.
Pineapple	Hot pack	Pints: 15 minutes Quarts: 20 minutes	Peel and core pineapple, and then cut into slices or cubes. Boil in a canning medium for 10 minutes.
Plums, halved or whole	Hot pack	Pints: 20 minutes Quarts: 25 minutes	Prick skins of plums. Halve and pit freestone varieties if desired. Boil in a canning medium for 2 minutes, and then cover and let stand for 20 minutes before packing in hot jars.
Rhubarb	Hot pack	Pints: 15 minutes Quarts: 15 minutes	Wash rhubarb and cut into 1/2-inch (1.25-cm) pieces. Place in a saucepan with 1/2 cup sugar for each quart of rhubarb. When liquid is drawn out, bring to a boil, and then pack in hot jars.

*Refer to "Boiling-Water Canning Processing Times" in Part 3 for altitude adjustment tables if you are more than 1,001 feet (305 m) above sea level. Your local government service organization or agricultural extension can let you know your altitude if you are unsure.

**Unless otherwise indicated, leave 1/2 inch (1.25 cm) headspace when canning fruits.

Canned Peaches

Peaches taste best when canned in medium syrup. Choose firm, ripe peaches for best quality, and use the hot-pack method to minimize issues with floating fruit.

For 9 pt.

11 lb. (5 kg) fresh peaches

Ascorbic acid solution (see "Preparing Fruits for Canning")

Simple syrup:

2 ¼ cups sugar

5 ¼ cups water

For 7 qt.

17 ½ lb. (8 kg) fresh peaches

Ascorbic acid solution (see "Preparing Fruits for Canning")

Simple syrup:

3 ¾ cups sugar

8 ¼ cups water

1. Blanch and peel peaches, remove pits, and cut into halves or slices. Dip in ascorbic acid solution, and drain immediately.

2. Stir sugar and water together in a large pot, and cook over medium heat, stirring frequently, until sugar is dissolved and mixture comes to a boil, about 10 minutes.

3. Carefully add peaches to simple syrup, and return to a boil. Reduce heat to medium-low, and cook for 5 minutes.

4. Pack hot peaches and simple syrup into prepared jars, leaving ½ inch (1.25 cm) headspace. Use a bubble remover to remove air bubbles by pressing gently around the fruit, and adjust headspace with more syrup if necessary. Wipe rims and affix lids.

5. In a boiling-water canner, process pints for 25 minutes and quarts for 30 minutes. Cool and store.

Variation: For *Lightly Spiced Peaches,* cut a 4-inch (10.25-cm) square of cheesecloth. Place 1 cinnamon stick and 1 star anise pod inside the cheesecloth, and tie in a small bundle. Make simple syrup with spice bundle, and then remove before canning.

Apricot Nectar

To can apricot halves or slices, follow the instructions for peaches (but don't peel them). Or try preserving the delicious, candy-like flavor of apricots in jars of sweet nectar. You can drink the bright-orange liquid as a juice or use it as a poaching liquid for winter fruits and compotes.

For 9 pt.

> 16 lb. (7.25 kg) fresh apricots
>
> Ascorbic acid solution (see "Preparing Fruits for Canning")
>
> Water
>
> Sugar (optional)

For 7 qt.

> 16 lb. (7.25 kg) fresh apricots
>
> Ascorbic acid solution (see "Preparing Fruits for Canning")
>
> Water
>
> Sugar (optional)

1. Halve apricots and remove pits. Dip in ascorbic acid solution, and drain immediately.

2. Measure apricots into a large pot, and add 1 cup water for every 4 cups fruit. Cook over medium heat until softened, about 10 minutes.

3. Run apricots through a food mill, and return to the pot. Taste, and add sugar to taste (if desired), up to ½ cup per quart or ¼ cup per pint. Return the mixture to a boil, and stir until sugar is dissolved, about 10 minutes.

4. Pack hot apricot nectar into prepared jars, leaving ½ inch (1.25 cm) headspace. Use a bubble remover to remove air bubbles by stirring gently, and adjust headspace if necessary. Wipe rims and affix lids.

5. In a boiling-water canner, process pints or quarts for 15 minutes. Cool and store.

Canned Sweet or Sour Cherries

Sweet cherries don't need the added sugar of simple syrup and can be simply canned in apple juice, while sour cherries taste best when canned in heavy syrup.

Floating Fruit

Is floating fruit getting you down? Don't be discouraged! It's normal to see fruit floating after the canning process, especially if you've used the raw-pack method or are canning a fruit with natural buoyancy due to a large amount of air in its cells. As the fruit sits in its canning medium, the sugars in the canning liquid and the cells of the fruit will equalize. You may find fruit that was floating on the day it was canned has settled after a week.

For 9 pt.

12 lb. (5.5 kg) fresh sweet or sour cherries

Ascorbic acid solution (see "Preparing Fruits for Canning")

Simple syrup:

3¼ cups sugar

5 cups water

or

2¼ cups apple juice

For 7 qt.

18 lb. (8.25 kg) fresh sweet or sour cherries

Ascorbic acid solution (see "Preparing Fruits for Canning")

Simple syrup:

5¼ cups sugar

7¾ cups water

or

3½ cups apple juice

1. Remove stems, and pit cherries if desired. If pitting, dip in ascorbic acid solution, and drain immediately. If you aren't pitting, poke each cherry with a sewing needle or small skewer to check skins.

2a. If canning in syrup, stir sugar and water together in a large pot, and cook over medium heat, stirring frequently, until sugar is dissolved and mixture comes to a boil.

2b. Heat apple juice in a large pot until boiling.

3. Add cherries to canning medium, and return to a boil.

4. Pack hot cherries into prepared jars, leaving ½ inch (1.25 cm) headspace. Use a bubble remover to remove air bubbles by pressing gently around fruit, and adjust headspace with more syrup if necessary. Wipe rims and affix lids.

5. In a boiling-water canner, process pints for 15 minutes and quarts for 20 minutes. Cool and store.

Canned Blueberries

Blueberries are easy to can using the raw-pack method, which helps to preserve their shape and texture. Plan on using about 5 cups berries (1¼ quarts) for each canned quart.

For 9 pt.
- 8 lb. (3.75 kg) fresh blueberries
- Simple syrup:
- 2¼ cups sugar
- 5¼ cups water

For 7 qt.
- 12 lb. (5.5 kg) fresh blueberries
- Simple syrup:
- 3¾ cups sugar
- 8¼ cups water

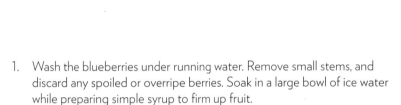

1. Wash the blueberries under running water. Remove small stems, and discard any spoiled or overripe berries. Soak in a large bowl of ice water while preparing simple syrup to firm up fruit.

2. Stir together sugar and water in a large pot, and cook over medium heat, stirring frequently, until sugar is dissolved and mixture comes to a boil, about 10 minutes.

3. Pack blueberries in prepared jars, leaving about ¾ inch (2 cm) headspace. Add hot syrup to each jar, leaving ½ inch (1.25 cm) headspace. Use a bubble remover to remove air bubbles, gently pressing around fruit to avoid crushing the berries, and then adjust headspace with more syrup if needed. Wipe jar rims and affix lids.

4. In a boiling-water canner, process pints for 20 minutes and quarts for 25 minutes. Cool and store.

Bubbling Fruit

Smaller fruits, such as berries and cherries, need more attention during the bubbling process than larger fruits, as there are so many more places for air bubbles to hide. Use your bubble remover or a plastic knife to gently press the fruit inward, working all the way around the jar, to be sure all the air bubbles have been released before canning.

Cinnamon Applesauce

Firm, tart apples may simply be peeled and hot packed in syrup or juice (see "Processing Times for Fruits"), but for a real treat, stir up a batch of cinnamon applesauce. My favorite applesauce is made with sweet apples, such as Delicious, Fuji, or Gala.

For 9 pt.

13^1/$_2$ lb. (6 kg) apples

Ascorbic acid solution (see "Preparing Fruits for Canning")

^{1}/$_2$ cup water or apple cider

1 TB. cinnamon

Up to 1 TB. granulated sugar per pint (optional)

For 7 qt.

21 lb. (9.5 kg) apples

Ascorbic acid solution (see "Preparing Fruits for Canning")

^{3}/$_4$ cup water

2 TB. cinnamon

Up to 2 TB. granulated sugar per pint (optional)

Canning Applesauce

Aim for the consistency of commercial applesauce. If it's too thick, add some apple cider to the finished sauce, and then return it to a boil before canning. Check seals carefully. If you must reprocess, return your applesauce to a boil in a saucepan, and start over with hot, clean jars and new lids.

1. Core and slice apples, dip in ascorbic acid solution, and drain immediately; there is no need to peel apples.

2. Heat apples and water or apple cider in a large pot over medium-high heat until soft, about 10 to 20 minutes.

3. Run apples through a food mill, and return to the pot. Stir in cinnamon, and return the mixture to a boil. Cook for 5 minutes, stirring gently. Remove from heat, and allow to rest for 5 minutes, stirring very gently once or twice before packing.

4. Pack hot applesauce into prepared jars, leaving ^{1}/$_2$ inch (1.25 cm) headspace. Use a bubble remover to remove air bubbles by stirring gently, and adjust headspace if necessary. Wipe rims and affix lids.

5. In a boiling-water canner, process pints for 20 minutes and quarts for 25 minutes. Cool and store.

Variation: For *Chunky Applesauce*, peel apples before heating. Mash to the desired consistency with a potato masher, and proceed with the recipe.

Canned Pear Halves

Pears are so delicious when canned in heavy syrup, you'll want to eat them straight from the jar! If you're concerned about sugar, substitute apple juice for the simple syrup.

For 9 pt.

11 lb. (5 kg) pears

Ascorbic acid solution (see "Preparing Fruits for Canning")

Simple syrup:

3¼ cups sugar

5 cups water

For 7 qt.

17½ lb. (8 kg) pears

Ascorbic acid solution (see "Preparing Fruits for Canning")

Simple syrup:

5¼ cups sugar

7¾ cups water

1. Blanch pears for 30 seconds to soften fruit and loosen skins, and then peel with a potato peeler. Use a melon baller or a grapefruit spoon to cut out core and seeds, dip in ascorbic acid solution, and drain immediately.

2. Stir together sugar and water in a large pot, and cook over medium heat, stirring frequently, until sugar is dissolved and mixture comes to a boil, about 10 minutes.

3. Add drained pear halves to simple syrup, and boil for 5 minutes.

4. Carefully pack hot pears and syrup into prepared jars, leaving ½ inch (1.25 cm) headspace. Use a bubble remover to remove air bubbles by stirring gently, and adjust headspace if necessary by adding more syrup. Wipe rims and affix lids.

5. In a boiling-water canner, process pints for 20 minutes and quarts for 25 minutes. Cool and store.

Variation: For *Canned Pears in Vanilla Syrup,* cut 1 vanilla bean in half lengthwise, and add to simple syrup ingredients. Remove and discard vanilla bean before packing fruit into jars.

Canned Whole Plums

If you dislike all the pitting and peeling that comes with most home-canning projects, you will love this easy method for preserving plums. Try small, clingstone varieties, such as Damson. A light syrup is all you need for plum-perfect results every time!

For 9 pt.

9 lb. (4 kg) small, clingstone plums

Simple syrup:

1½ cups sugar

5¾ cups water

For 7 qt.

14 lb. (6.25 kg) small, clingstone plums

Simple syrup:

2¼ cups sugar

9 cups water

1. Check the skins when canning whole, skin-on fruits, using a fork to prick both sides of each plum.

2. Stir together sugar and water in a large pot, and cook over medium heat, stirring frequently, until sugar is dissolved and mixture comes to a boil, about 10 minutes.

3. Add whole plums to simple syrup, and boil for 2 minutes. Turn off heat, cover pot, and let stand for 20 minutes.

4. Carefully pack hot plums and syrup into prepared jars, leaving ½ inch (1.25 cm) headspace. Use a bubble remover to remove air bubbles by stirring gently, and adjust headspace if necessary by adding more syrup. Wipe rims and affix lids.

5. In a boiling-water canner, process pints for 25 minutes and quarts for 30 minutes. Cool and store.

Variation: If you have freestone plums that are easily pitted, simply halve plums, remove pits, and proceed with the recipe.

Canned Orange and Grapefruit Sections

Citrus fruits need little more than water to make an excellent and nutritious canned product. Try mixing different citrus fruits for a beautiful appearance and delicious flavor.

For 9 pt.

13 lb. (6 kg) mixed oranges and grapefruit
Boiling water

For 7 qt.

15 lb. (6.75 kg) mixed oranges and grapefruit
Boiling water

1. Cut away peel and pith of oranges and grapefruit.

2. Hold fruit in your palm and carefully cut between membranes to release individual segments, working over a bowl to catch any juices that are released. Squeeze remaining membrane structure after segments are released to collect any remaining juice.

3. Pack oranges and grapefruit firmly without crushing in prepared jars, leaving about ¾ inch (2 cm) headspace. Add any collected juice, and then fill jars with boiling water, leaving ½ inch (1.25 cm) headspace.

4. Use a bubble remover to remove air bubbles by stirring gently, and adjust headspace if necessary by adding more water. Wipe rims and affix lids.

5. In a boiling-water canner, process pints for 10 minutes and quarts for 15 minutes. Cool and store.

Thickened Fillings

If you'd like a thick, pie-ready filling, ClearJel is the only thickener that's safe to use. ClearJel is a modified food starch used in commercial canning and baking that holds fillings together without overthickening or thinning out during storage. Fillings made with ClearJel are thickened to the proper consistency, allowing heat penetration to destroy potential spoilers.

You can find ClearJel in 1-pound (453.5-g) packages online and in some stores. Be sure you purchase *regular,* not *instant,* ClearJel, as the instant variety is an institutional product not recommended for home canning.

Thickener-Free Fillings

If you prefer, you can can your pie fillings without thickener and add 1 tablespoon flour, tapioca, or cornstarch to each quart just before baking. A filling canned without ClearJel will be looser and has the potential to separate when stored.

Making Pie Fillings

With a few quarts of homemade pie filling in your pantry, you'll be ready to whip up a delicious, homemade pie in the amount of time it takes to roll out the crust!

What You'll Need

Treatment solution	ClearJel (if using)
Jars	Sugar
Lids and seals	Spices (if using)
Canner	Saucepan
Fruit	Bottled lemon juice
Pot or blancher	Jar funnel
Ice bath (if needed)	Bubble remover
Apple peeler/corer or paring knife	Kitchen towels

Before You Begin

1. Prepare treatment solution
If you are canning a fruit prone to browning, prepare a treatment solution (see "Preparing Fruits for Canning").

2. Prepare jars, lids, and canner
Prepare your jars, lids, and canner as outlined in "Preparing the Jars and Equipment." Keep the jars and lids at a simmer until ready to use.

For Safety's Sake

A quick online search will yield many pie filling recipes, but beware. Both the USDA and the National Center for Home Food Preservation advise against thickening pie fillings with cornstarch, flour, or tapioca before canning. While the acidity of the fruit will prevent the growth of botulism, other dangerous spoilers can grow within improperly canned fillings due to increased viscosity, and—contrary to conventional wisdom—spices such as cinnamon will not inhibit spoilage. Remember, just because a recipe hasn't sickened somebody *yet* doesn't mean it's safe; use tested recipes and approved methods.

1: Wash fruit
Wash fruit in plenty of cold, running water. Check fruit for soft spots or blemishes.

2. Blanch, peel, slice, and treat
Refer to the "Preparing Fruits for Canning" for detailed instructions for each fruit.

Blanch peaches and pears before peeling, then submerge in an ice bath to loosen skin. For apples, peel with an apple peeler/corer. Dip fruits prone to browning in treatment solution, and drain.

3. Mix, add liquids, and heat
Combine ClearJel, sugar, and spices in a saucepan, and stir well. Add any juice or water, and cook over medium-low heat, stirring constantly, until thick and bubbly. Stir in bottled lemon juice just before you add the fruit.

Making Pie Fillings

4. Add fruit
Gently fold fruit into bubbling mixture. Reduce heat to a simmer to keep mixture hot while packing jars.

5. Pack jars
Using a jar funnel, ladle hot filling into hot, prepared jars, leaving 1 inch (2.5 cm) headspace.

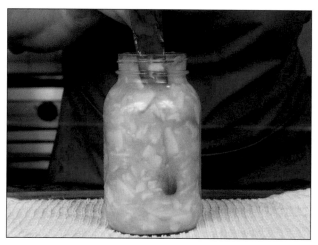

6. Remove bubbles and check headspace
Run a bubble remover around the edges of fruit, gently pressing inward so no pockets of air remain. Using the opposite side of the bubble remover, check headspace on each jar. Add or remove filling if necessary.

7. Clean jar rims and affix lids
Use a clean kitchen towel and hot water to wipe the edge of each jar, removing every speck of food and syrup. Place a hot lid on each jar, and screw bands to fingertip tightness.

8. Place jars in canner

Place filled jars in the canning rack and gently submerge them in the simmering water. Put the lid on the pot, and turn heat to the highest setting.

9. Process jars

When water has come to a boil and steam begins to escape from the lid, begin timing according to the recipe. After that has ended, turn off the heat, and leave jars in the canner for 5 minutes.

10. Remove jars, cool, and store

Remove carefully, and set on a heatproof surface lined with kitchen towels for 24 hours. After 24 hours, wipe jars clean or rinse under room-temperature running water. Check seals carefully, and store for up to 2 years.

Peach Pie Filling

Enjoy the fresh taste of summer peaches all year long. This filling makes a delicious pie, cobbler, or crumble. Each 1-quart jar will make a 9-inch (22.75-cm) pie.

For 1 qt.

3^1/$_2$ cups fresh peaches

Ascorbic acid solution (see "Preparing Fruits for Canning")

^{3}/$_4$ cup cold water

1 cup granulated sugar

^{1}/$_4$ tsp. ground cinnamon (optional)

^{1}/$_4$ cup ClearJel

^{1}/$_4$ cup bottled lemon juice

For 7 qt.

17^1/$_2$ lb. (8 kg) fresh peaches

Ascorbic acid solution (see "Preparing Fruits for Canning")

5^1/$_4$ cups cold water

7 cups granulated sugar

1 tsp. ground cinnamon (optional)

2 cups ClearJel

1^3/$_4$ cups bottled lemon juice

1. Blanch and peel peaches, remove pits, and slice ^{1}/$_2$ inch (1.25 cm) thick. Dip in ascorbic acid solution, and drain immediately.

2. Bring a large pot of water to a rolling boil. Drop in peach slices, working a few cups at a time, and cook for 1 minute after water returns to a boil. Keep warm while cooking remaining peaches.

3. Combine water, sugar, cinnamon (if using), and ClearJel in a large pot, and bring to a boil. Cook until mixture is thick and nearly boiling, stirring almost constantly, about 5 minutes.

4. Add bottled lemon juice, and bring mixture to a boil. Carefully fold in peach slices, and cook, stirring constantly, until mixture is set, about 1 minute.

5. Pack hot peach pie filling into sterilized quart jars, attach lids and bands, and process for 35 minutes. Cool completely, and store.

Filling Helpful Hint

I find that a large, heatproof silicone spatula is the perfect tool for stirring and packing pie filling, as it allows you to scrape every last bit of gelled filling from the inside of your pot.

Apricot Pie Filling

Apricots hold a beautiful, firm texture when canned into pie filling, and you don't have to peel them first! Try this pie filling with a buttery crumb topping for a luscious treat.

For 1 qt.

5 cups fresh apricots

Ascorbic acid solution (see "Preparing Fruits for Canning")

1 cup cold water

1 cup granulated sugar

$1/4$ tsp. freshly grated nutmeg

$1/4$ cup ClearJel

2 TB. bottled lemon juice

$1/4$ tsp. almond extract

For 7 qt.

14 lb. (6.25 kg) fresh apricots

Ascorbic acid solution (see "Preparing Fruits for Canning")

8 cups cold water

8 cups granulated sugar

2 tsp. freshly grated nutmeg

2 cups ClearJel

1 cup bottled lemon juice

2 tsp. almond extract

1. Slice large apricots $1/2$ inch (1.25 cm) thick, or halve small apricots, removing pits as you work. Dip fruit in ascorbic acid solution to prevent browning, and drain immediately.

2. Combine cold water, sugar, nutmeg, and ClearJel in a large pot, and bring to a boil. Cook until mixture is thick and nearly boiling, about 5 minutes.

3. Add bottled lemon juice and almond extract, and bring mixture to a boil. Carefully stir in apricots, and cook, stirring constantly, until mixture is thick and filling has set, about 1 minute.

4. Pack apricot pie filling into sterilized quart jars, attach lids and bands, and process for 35 minutes. Cool completely, and store.

Working with ClearJel

ClearJel sets fillings quickly. Some people love the thick, sweet flavor of thickened pie fillings, while other families may enjoy a thinner filling. Start with the 1-quart recipes and see if you like it. If you find it too thick, you can safely halve the amount of ClearJel in the recipe for a looser set.

Blueberry Pie Filling

Tiny wild blueberries make an incredible filling, but cultivated blueberries are a delicious treat, too.

For 1 qt.

4 cups fresh wild or cultivated blueberries

Ascorbic acid solution (see "Preparing Fruits for Canning")

1 cup cold water

1 cup granulated sugar

⅛ tsp. cinnamon

¼ cup ClearJel

2 TB. bottled lemon juice

Blue food coloring (optional)

For 7 qt.

24 cups (6 qt.) fresh wild or cultivated blueberries

Ascorbic acid solution (see "Preparing Fruits for Canning")

6 cups cold water

6 cups granulated sugar

1 tsp. cinnamon

1¾ cups ClearJel

¾ cup bottled lemon juice

Blue food coloring (optional)

1. Wash and pick over blueberries, removing any stems and discarding bruised or crushed berries.

2. Combine cold water, sugar, cinnamon, and ClearJel in a large pot, and bring to a boil. Cook until mixture is thick and nearly boiling, about 5 minutes.

3. Add bottled lemon juice, and bring mixture to a boil. Carefully stir in blueberries, add a few drops of blue food coloring (if using), and cook for 1 minute. Remove from heat.

4. Pack blueberry pie filling into sterilized quart jars. Wipe rims, attach prepared lids and bands, and process for 35 minutes. Cool completely, and store.

Tips for Successful Pie Fillings

Pie filling can be challenging. ClearJel thickens recipes quickly, and fruit fillings are notoriously persnickety to can. Follow these tips to ensure success every time:

- Start small—make 1 quart of pie filling on your first try, rather than a big batch.

- If you find the filling too thick, reduce the amount of ClearJel, or eliminate it entirely if you like a loose filling.

- Blanch fruit before making filling. Fruit has quite a bit of air in the cells, so blanching or heating it first will eliminate bubbling over in jars.

- Remove air bubbles carefully. Be vigilant when removing air bubbles to prevent jars from bubbling over.

- Measure headspace carefully! Don't eyeball it; use the measuring tool on your jar bubbler or a ruler.

- Don't double the recipe. It's essential to process the filling while it's very hot, and ClearJel thickens the filling significantly. If you try to make a 14-quart batch, quality will be iffy, and you may have trouble stirring it.

- Keep canner water at a simmer. Aim to place the jars in 180°F (82°C) water for a fast boil.

- Try leaving the jars in the canner for 10 minutes before removing them to cool. The added pressure will help to seal the jars and eliminate oozing.

- Expect a learning curve! If jars ooze and bubble over, put them in the fridge and use for pie or turnovers within the next few days. If you still want to preserve it, freeze the finished, unbaked pie or turnovers.

Part 5

Jams, Jellies, and Preserves

What's more beautiful than a pantry shelf filled with fruit preserves, jellies, jams, fruit butters, chutneys, and marmalades? Open a jar of strawberry preserves to taste summer on a cold winter's day. Tuck a homemade jar of jam into a basket of freshly baked muffins for a beautiful and heartfelt homemade gift. Enjoy the satisfaction of creating the perfect grape or apple jelly. These techniques are easy to learn, so jump right in!

All About Jams, Jellies, and Preserves

Jams, preserves, jellies, marmalades, fruit butters, and conserves are all gelled products. To create them, specific quantities of fruit, sugar, acid, and sometimes added pectin are cooked to a temperature at which liquid becomes a gel.

Unlike the canning process for whole fruits, gelled products are a good use for fruits that are slightly over- or underripe, and therefore unsuitable for canning or freezing. While you'll still achieve the most perfect results from perfectly ripe, seasonal fruit, jams and jellies are more forgiving. The higher pectin levels in underripe fruit help to create a gel, and the process of crushing or juicing the fruit means the less-beautiful specimens will still find a way into your pantry. When working with less-than-perfect fruit, aim for a mix of 75 percent ripe fruit to 25 percent underripe fruit.

Types of Gelled Fruit Spreads

All gelled products are preserved by sugar, but each is a bit different:

Jelly is a classic American spread prepared by cooking fruit juice with sugar (and sometimes added pectin) to a clear or translucent, wobbly, tender gel.

Jam is both juice and puréed fruit that has been cooked with sugar (and sometimes added pectin) to a thick, spreadable consistency. **Preserves** are nearly the same as jam, but the fruit is left whole or in larger chunks. The word *preserves* is often used interchangeably with jam.

Fruit butter is a thick, smooth spread created by cooking fruit until soft, running it through a sieve or food mill, and cooking it again with sugar until it can be mounded on a spoon.

Marmalade is a fruit preserve made from the juice and peel of citrus fruits.

Conserves are fruit preserves made from tender fruits cooked quickly with sugar, nuts, and sometimes dried fruit.

Tips for Success

Gelling is a chemical reaction, but success is guaranteed if you follow instructions carefully when making gelled products. Measure carefully, use tested recipes, and never double a recipe. Doubling recipes for gelled products will result in a runny, undercooked product or an overcooked, caramelized mess. If you love a particular jam or jelly and want to have a big batch on hand, make it twice.

When jams and jellies without added pectin are cooked for long periods of time, bubbles can form and fruit can float. As you learned in Part 4, "Canning Fruits," floating fruit makes an undesirable (but still edible) product. Avoid this issue by taking your jam off the heat at regular intervals and stirring it for 1 minute before returning it to the heat. This will eliminate air bubbles and prevent floating fruit.

Always use fresh fruit when making naturally gelled products. Commercially produced juices do not contain enough pectin because processing breaks down natural pectin. If you want to can with juice and added pectin, use a recipe that was developed for that purpose.

Finally, be careful not to overcook your fruit spreads. Stir frequently, and add water when the recipe calls for it.

All About Pectin

Remember when you asked your science teacher, "When am I going to use this information in real life?" The answer is now. Creating gelled products requires the use of biology and chemistry, but don't be intimidated. Jams, jellies, and other gelled products are among the most fun and trouble-free foods to can!

Pectin is a naturally occurring soluble fiber that binds plant cells together. There are two types of pectin in plant cells. One holds the cells themselves together, and the other is present within the walls of the cell.

While pectin is present in all fruits, some have more than others. Acid is also a factor, as a proper balance of acid to pectin is necessary to create a gel. Pectin levels drop as food ripens, so using some underripe fruit can increase the overall pectin level of a recipe.

Gelled products can be made with or without added pectin. Some fruits are more suited to pectin-free cookery than others, and many home canners prefer the unadulterated nature of naturally gelled fruit spreads. The benefits of using added pectin appeal to some—fully ripe fruit can be used; the cooking time is shorter; and yields are higher, as the volume of fruit is not reduced during long cooking.

The following chart provides a general guideline for pectin levels in commonly used fruits. You will eventually get a feel for what needs pectin and what doesn't. I have always canned my berry and apricot jams without added pectin, as I don't mind the unpredictable consistency and prefer the pure fruit flavor that results from a naturally cooked jam. If you're going to experiment, just go into it with the mindset that sometimes things won't work out the way you planned. Some of my earlier, experimental batches went into the freezer and ended up as ice cream toppings, soda syrups, or cake ingredients. If you want perfect results every time, follow tested recipes!

Pectin Levels in Commonly Used Fruits

Optimal Pectin and Acid Levels—Will Gel When Cooked with Sugar	Borderline Levels of Acid or Pectin	Low Levels of Acid, Pectin, or Both
Apples, tart	Apples, very ripe	Apricots
Blackberries, tart	Blackberries, very ripe	Blueberries
Crabapples	Cherries, sour	Cherries, sweet
Cranberries	Elderberries	Figs
Currants, red	Grape juice, bottled, Eastern Concord	Grapes, Western Concord
Gooseberries	Grapefruit	Nectarines
Grapes, Eastern Concord	Grapes, California	Peaches
Lemons	Oranges	Pears
Plums (except Italian)		Pineapple
Quinces		Plums, Italian prune
		Raspberries
		Rhubarb
		Strawberries

Testing Pectin Levels

If you have a large batch of fruit and are unsure whether it has enough pectin and acid to gel, there are two ways to find out. The appropriate level of pectin and acid is most important when making jellies; other preparations are more forgiving.

The cooking test: Measure $1/3$ cup juice and $1/4$ cup sugar into a small saucepan, and stir over low heat to dissolve sugar. Turn heat to high, and boil until the mixture "sheets" off a spoon (see "Testing Gel Stages"). Pour the mixture onto a small plate, and let cool. If the mixture forms a gel, the fruit does not require added pectin.

The alcohol test: Place 1 teaspoon juice in a small jar with 1 tablespoon rubbing alcohol. Do not taste—this mixture is poisonous! Put the lid on and shake the jar gently. If the fruit juice forms a solid, jellylike mass, the fruit does not require added pectin.

Using a Jelmeter

If you are an advanced home canner or own a fruit farm or home-based business, a Jelmeter may be a good purchase. A Jelmeter is a graduated glass tube with a small opening that can help you determine how much sugar you need to use with a fruit. Boil fruit juice for 10 minutes, and then cool to room temperature. Fill the Jelmeter with juice, and allow it to flow through the narrow opening for 1 minute. Markings on the Jelmeter indicate the amount of sugar to use with 1 cup juice.

Types of Pectin

There are many types of commercial pectin available. Use tested recipes when adding pectin, and always refer to the instructions included in the box. Many types of pectin are available in your local supermarket. Use the type specified in the recipe you're using—they're not interchangeable.

- Commercial fruit pectins are made from apples or citrus and are available in liquid or powdered form in classic (with sugar) and low- or no-sugar formulas. Always use the type called for in your recipe.

- Low-methoxyl (no-sugar-needed) pectins are extracted from citrus using a different method, which creates a pectin that requires little or no added sugar to form a gel.

- Instant, freezer, or no-cook pectins are made especially for making freezer jam, in which the fruit is cooked very little or not at all.

Testing Gel Stages

Jams, jellies, and preserves are referred to as *gelled products*. It is important to cook them to the correct consistency in order to form a gel, rather than a syrup with fruit floating in it. It's particularly important when working without added pectin to test the liquid to see when it has reached the gel point (the point at which a jam or jelly has "set" into a gelled form).

When cooking with commercial pectin, it's best to follow the instructions provided with your particular product. Some foods will gel more quickly, and each product works a bit differently.

The following are three ways to test whether your jam, jelly, or preserves have gelled.

Temperature Test

The temperature test is the most accurate way to know you've reached the gel point. To do this, use a candy thermometer, and stop cooking as soon as it reaches 8 degrees above the boiling point, usually 220°F (104°C). Use the temperature test when making any kind of jams, jellies, or preserves. For perfect jelly, the temperature test is the only 100 percent accurate test.

Test your thermometer for accuracy before you begin by using it to bring a small saucepan of water to a boil. If the temperature reads 212°F (100°C) when the water boils, your thermometer is accurate.

If you live at an altitude of more than 1,000 feet (305 m) above sea level, your water boils at a lower temperature, and the gel point must therefore be adjusted. Water will boil at 210°F (99°C) at 2,000 feet (610 m) above sea level, so the gel point is 218°F (103°C). For each 1,000 feet (305 m) above sea level, subtract 2 degrees. For absolute precision, test your thermometer with boiling water, determine the boiling point at your altitude, and add 8 degrees.

An Imperfect Science

When making jelly, I like to use more than one method to check for the gel point. I always use a properly calibrated thermometer and am a big fan of the refrigerator test. For quick results, I keep a batch of soup spoons in the freezer. When I'm ready to test, I spoon a little jelly onto the chilled spoon and pop it back in the freezer; it will set very quickly if the jelly is ready. I have found that the sheet test is an imperfect science— sometimes all other factors indicate the gel point, and the jelly still won't sheet off the darned spoon! Trust your gut (and your thermometer) when testing gel points. With a little practice, you'll make perfect jelly every time.

Refrigerator Test

The refrigerator test is an acceptable method for testing jams and preserves, as there is generally more leeway in cooking times with these products. After boiling for a few minutes, remove the jam or preserves mixture from the heat, spoon a small amount onto a clean plate or soup spoon, and place it in the freezer for 2 to 3 minutes. If the mixture gels and wrinkles when you push it with your finger, it's done.

Spoon or Sheet Test

When making jelly without a candy thermometer, the spoon or sheet test can provide a good idea of when the gel point is reached. Dip a cool metal spoon in the jelly mixture, lift the spoon, and turn it so the jelly runs off the side. When the gel point has been reached, the liquid will form two drops that flow together into one single sheet.

Making Traditional Jam, Preserves, Conserves, and Marmalade

You'll find that jam and preserves are the easiest and most forgiving of canning projects. Just gather your ingredients, cook, and can!

What You'll Need

Jars	Saucepan
Lids and seals	Potato masher
Canner	Jar funnel
Fruit	Bubble remover
Paring knife	Kitchen towels
Sugar	

Before You Begin

1. Sterilize canning jars
See Part 3, "Canning Food Basics," for complete instructions.

Because jams, jellies, and preserves are normally processed for less than 10 minutes, wash jars and then sterilize them by boiling in a canner for 10 minutes.

2. Prepare jars, lids, and canner
Prepare your jars, lids, and canner as outlined in Part 3, "Canning Food Basics." Keep jars and lids on simmer until ready to use.

1. Wash fruit
Wash fruit in plenty of cold, running water.

2. Trim
Check fruit for soft spots or blemishes, and trim away. Reserve very soft or overripe fruit for immediate consumption.

3. Prepare fruit
Slice fruit as directed in the recipe. Hull strawberries, and remove pits from stone fruits. Peel if desired. Fruit may be finely chopped before cooking, or mashed with a potato masher during the cooking process.

4. Mix fruit and sugar

Before you turn the heat on, gently stir fruit and sugar together in a large saucepan.

5. Cook to dissolve sugar

Cook over low heat, stirring to dissolve sugar. For a smooth, jamlike consistency, mash with a potato masher while cooking; for a chunkier preserve, simply stir. Gently bring fruit and sugar mixture to a boil, stirring occasionally.

Prepare Fruit by Hand!

It seems like an easy solution, but never use mechanical appliances, such as blenders, food processors, or juicers, to prepare fruit for gelled products. To preserve pectin levels in fruit, it must be gently prepared by hand. The mechanical action of these appliances will destroy pectin and mix air into the fruit, creating a sloppy mess instead of a sparkling jam, jelly, or preserve.

! *Don't forget to stir the corners of the pan!*

6. Boil mixture

Once sugar is dissolved, increase heat to medium-high to bring mixture to a rapid boil. Cook until thick and "jammy," stirring frequently to prevent scorching.

7. Test for gel point

Use one of the methods outlined in "Testing Gel Stages" to determine whether jam is ready. Remove jam from heat while testing.

8. Skim foam
Quickly skim away any foam that has formed during the cooking process.

9. Pack jars
Using a jar funnel, ladle jam or preserves into hot, sterilized jars. Use a bubble remover to remove air bubbles, and leave ¼ inch (.75 cm) headspace.

10. Clean jar rims and affix lids
Use a clean kitchen towel and hot water to wipe the edge of each jar, removing every speck of food and syrup. Place a hot lid on each jar, and screw bands to fingertip tightness.

11. Place jars in canner
Place filled jars in the canning rack, and gently submerge them in the simmering water. Put the lid on the pot, and turn heat to the highest setting.

12. Process jars
When water has come to a boil and steam begins to escape from the lid, set a timer for the amount of time specified in the recipe. After that time, turn off the heat, remove canner lid, and let jars rest for 5 minutes.

13. Cool and store jars
Remove jars carefully, and set on a heatproof surface lined with kitchen towels for 24 hours. Check seals carefully, and wipe jars clean or rinse under room-temperature running water. Store for up to 2 years.

Traditional Strawberry Jam

All you need are perfectly ripe, sweet strawberries and sugar to create this delicious jam. Strawberry jam is fantastic in bar cookies, doughnuts, or simply spread on toast.

Yield: About 6 to 8 half-pints

3 lb. (1.5 kg) strawberries, washed and hulled

6 cups granulated sugar

1. Place strawberries and sugar in a large, heavy-bottomed pot over medium heat. Cook over low heat, stirring frequently, until sugar is dissolved. Use a potato masher to crush strawberries.

2. Increase heat to medium-high, and bring mixture to a boil. Stir frequently, and then constantly as jam becomes thicker. For the most accurate results, use a candy thermometer, and cook jam to 220°F (104°C), or use the refrigerator test outlined in "Testing Pectin Levels." When jam is ready, it will look thick and "jammy." This can take up to 30 minutes, so be patient.

3. Using a canning funnel, ladle jam into sterilized half-pint jars, leaving ¼ inch (.75 cm) headspace. Use a bubble remover to remove air pockets, and adjust headspace if necessary. Wipe jar rims and affix two-piece lids.

4. Process for 5 minutes in a boiling-water canner. At the end of the processing time, turn off the heat, and let the canner stand, uncovered, for 5 minutes.

5. Remove jars to cooling racks or several layers of kitchen towels, and cool for 24 hours before checking seals and storing.

Traditional Apricot Jam

Apricots need a little extra acid in order to gel, so lemon juice is added to this recipe. Apricot jam is amazing on a danish!

Yield: About 6 to 8 half-pints

3 lb. (1.5 kg) fresh apricots

½ cup bottled or fresh lemon juice

6 cups granulated sugar

1. Blanch, peel, halve, and pit apricots. Place in a large pot with lemon juice and sugar, and cook over low heat, stirring frequently, until sugar is dissolved. Use a potato masher to crush apricots into a chunky purée.

2. Increase heat to medium-high, and bring mixture to a boil. Stir frequently, and then constantly as jam becomes thicker. For the most accurate results, use a candy thermometer, and cook jam to 220°F (104°C), or use the refrigerator test outlined in "Testing Pectin Levels." When jam is ready, after approximately 30 minutes, it will look thick and "jammy."

3. Using a canning funnel, ladle jam into sterilized half-pint jars, leaving ¼ inch (.75 cm) headspace. Use a bubble remover to remove air pockets, and adjust headspace if necessary. Wipe jar rims and affix two-piece lids.

4. Process for 5 minutes in a boiling-water canner. At the end of the processing time, turn off the heat, and let the canner stand, uncovered, for 5 minutes.

5. Remove jars to cooling racks or several layers of kitchen towels, and cool for 24 hours before checking seals and storing.

No-Cook Peach Freezer Jam

Want to make jam but hate to heat up the kitchen? Try this easy freezer jam. Be sure to use "no-cook" pectin for a quick set and desirable consistency.

Yield: About 6 to 8 half-pints

5 cups fresh peaches, blanched, peeled, and crushed

$1/4$ cup bottled or fresh lemon juice

6 cups granulated sugar

1 pkg. no-cook powdered pectin

Freezer Jams

I like to call freezer jam "the lazy canner's jam," because it requires almost no work at all. Of course, there's always a price to pay, and in this case, it's the increased sweetness from added pectin and the looser consistency of the uncooked jams and preserves. Expect freezer jams to have a "spoonable" texture rather than the tightly gelled set of traditional jam.

1. Blanch and peel peaches, and put them in a large bowl. Use a potato masher to mash them with bottled lemon juice into a chunky purée.

2. Whisk sugar and powdered pectin together in a medium bowl, making sure there are no lumps.

3. Stir sugar into peaches, mixing well. Let stand, stirring every 5 minutes, until sugar has dissolved and jam begins to set, about 30 minutes. Skim jam if necessary.

4. Ladle jam into washed and dried freezer containers or half-pint jars, leaving $1/2$ inch (1.25 cm) headspace. Let stand at room temperature for several hours until set.

5. Pack in freezer-safe containers with 1 inch (2.5 cm) headspace, and freeze.

Blueberry Freezer Jam

Traditional (classic) pectin can be used in freezer jam, but the finished product will need to sit at room temperature for 24 hours to set properly. Allow for extra time.

Yield: About 6 to 8 half-pints

2 qt. (about 8 cups) fresh or frozen blueberries

4 cups granulated sugar

2 TB. bottled or fresh lemon juice

1 pkg. classic powdered pectin

$1/2$ cup water

1. Stir blueberries, sugar, and lemon juice together in a large bowl.

2. Whisk pectin and water together in a small saucepan over medium heat, and bring to a boil.

3. Pour pectin mixture over blueberries, and stir until sugar has completely dissolved, about 10 minutes. Cover, and let stand at room temperature for up to 24 hours, until jam has set into a spoonable gel. Skim jam if necessary.

4. Ladle jam into washed and dried freezer containers or half-pint jars, leaving 1 inch (2.5 cm) headspace. Freeze.

Pineapple Jam (with Pectin)

Pineapples are a low-pectin fruit that will not gel without some help. Liquid pectin makes a perfect set every time. This recipe is the perfect choice for beginners and can even be made with canned pineapple.

Yield: About 4 half-pints

$2^{1}/_{2}$ cups or 1 (20-oz.) can fresh pineapple, crushed

3 TB. bottled or fresh lemon juice

$3^{1}/_{2}$ cups granulated sugar

1 pkg. liquid pectin

No-Sugar-Added Jam

It's easy to make your favorite jams and preserves with no sugar added—just be sure that the pectin you're purchasing is labeled "low sugar" or "no sugar needed," and follow the instructions provided with the box. To make no-sugar jams, be sure to use pectin, or you'll have to cook the fruit for so long that it will caramelize and produce an unpleasant flavor and color.

1. Heat crushed pineapple and lemon juice in a heavy-bottomed saucepan. Add sugar, and bring to a boil, stirring constantly. Boil for 1 minute over high heat. Remove from heat.

2. Gently stir in liquid pectin. Skim any foam that has accumulated on the top of jam.

3. Using a canning funnel, ladle jam into sterilized half-pint jars, leaving $^{1}/_{4}$ inch (.75 cm) headspace. Use a bubble remover to remove air pockets, and adjust headspace if necessary. Wipe jar rims and affix two-piece lids.

4. Process for 5 minutes in a boiling-water canner. At the end of the processing time, turn off the heat and let the canner stand, uncovered, for 5 minutes.

5. Remove jars to cooling racks or several layers of kitchen towels, and cool for 24 hours before checking seals and storing.

Mixed-Berry Jam (with Pectin)

Blackberries, blueberries, and raspberries combine with powdered pectin to make an easy, delicious jam with a big batch yield.

Yield: About 11 to 12 half-pints

6 cups crushed blackberries, blueberries, and raspberries (about 1 qt.-sized box of each)

1 pkg. powdered pectin

8 cups granulated sugar

1. If desired, press crushed berries through a food mill or strainer to remove seeds before measuring. Stir together with powdered pectin in a large, heavy-bottomed pot, and bring to a boil over high heat.

2. Stir in sugar, and return to a boil. Boil hard for 1 minute, stirring gently and continuously.

3. Using a canning funnel, ladle jam into sterilized half-pint jars, leaving $1/4$ inch (.75 cm) headspace. Use a bubble remover to remove air pockets, and adjust headspace if necessary. Wipe jar rims and affix two-piece lids.

4. Process for 5 minutes in a boiling-water canner. At the end of the processing time, turn off the heat and let the canner stand, uncovered, for 5 minutes.

5. Remove jars to cooling racks or several layers of kitchen towels, and cool for 24 hours before checking seals and storing.

Frozen Fruit

This recipe yields fantastic results when made with frozen fruit. My local warehouse store sells big bags of organic frozen mixed berries, so I can make big batches of this jam to give as gifts all year round. Let the berries thaw a bit so you can easily crush them with a potato masher, and then proceed with the recipe.

Part 5: Jams, Jellies, and Preserves

Valencia Orange–Ginger Marmalade

Sweet Valencia oranges are accented with a touch of ginger in this delicious, candylike marmalade that cooks down beautifully without added pectin.

Yield: About 6 to 7 half-pints

4 lb. (1.75 kg) Valencia oranges

1 cup water

1 TB. freshly grated ginger

4 cups granulated sugar

1. Use a citrus zester or potato peeler to remove peels of 6 oranges, leaving most but not all of white pith attached to orange. If using a peeler, slice peel into thin ribbons. To segment oranges, cut away pith (and peel, for remaining oranges), and then hold orange in your palm and carefully cut between membranes to release individual segments, working over a bowl to collect any juices that drain as you segment it.

2. Bring orange peel and water to a boil over high heat in a small saucepan. Cook for 3 minutes, and then drain.

3. Stir orange peel, oranges, collected juices, grated ginger, and sugar together in a heavy-bottomed pot over medium-low heat until sugar is dissolved, about 10 minutes. Increase heat to medium-high, and cook, stirring almost constantly, until marmalade reaches 220°F (104°C) on a candy thermometer, or passes the refrigerator gel test (see "Testing Gel Stages"), approximately 30 minutes.

4. Using a canning funnel, ladle marmalade into sterilized half pint jars, leaving 1/4 inch (.75 cm) headspace. Use a bubble remover to remove air pockets, and adjust headspace if necessary. Wipe jar rims and affix two-piece lids.

5. Process for 5 minutes in a boiling-water canner. At the end of the processing time, turn off the heat, and let the canner stand, uncovered, for 5 minutes.

6. Remove jars to cooling racks or several layers of kitchen towels, and cool for 24 hours before checking seals and storing.

Variation: For *Three-Citrus Marmalade,* use 2 pounds (907.25 g) Valencia oranges, 1 1/2 pounds (680.5 g) grapefruit, and 1/2 pound (226.75 g) Meyer lemons. Zest 1 of each fruit, and proceed with recipe.

Cranberry Conserve

Cranberries combine with citrus, tiny dried currants, and walnuts for a sweet, spoonable conserve that is fit for the Thanksgiving table.

Yield: About 3 to 4 half-pints

2 Meyer lemons or 1 orange, unpeeled and finely chopped

1 cup water

4 cups fresh or frozen cranberries

3 cups sugar

$1/2$ cup dried currants

$1/2$ cup chopped walnuts

1. Bring chopped lemon or orange and water to a boil over high heat in a medium, heavy-bottomed saucepan. Cook over medium heat until peel is tender, about 20 minutes.

2. Add cranberries, sugar, walnuts, and currants. Increase heat to medium-high, and cook, stirring almost constantly, until mixture reaches 220°F (104°C) on a candy thermometer, or passes the refrigerator gel test (see "Testing Gel Stages"), about 30 minutes.

3. Using a canning funnel, ladle conserve into prepared half-pint jars, leaving $1/4$ inch (.75 cm) headspace. Use a bubble remover to remove air pockets, and adjust headspace if necessary. Wipe jar rims and affix two-piece lids.

4. Process for 10 minutes in a boiling-water canner. At the end of the processing time, turn off the heat and let the canner stand, uncovered, for 5 minutes.

5. Remove jars to cooling racks or several layers of kitchen towels, and cool for 24 hours before checking seals and storing.

Variation: Replace cranberries with 5 cups Concord grapes. Halve and gently crush grapes, cook for 10 minutes, and run through a sieve to remove seeds before adding to recipe.

Cranberry Conserve

Preparing Jellies

A truly excellent jelly is tender, a bit jiggly, and clear. The quality of your jelly is determined by the quality of your juice; therefore, follow instructions carefully during the juice extraction process, and be sure to cook it to the exact temperature necessary for gelling.

What You'll Need

Jars

Lids and seals

Canner

Fruit

Paring knife

Jelly bag with stand or cheesecloth and mesh strainer

Potato masher

Saucepans

Candy thermometer or metal spoons

Jar funnel

Bubble remover

Kitchen towels

Before You Begin

1. Sterilize canning jars
See Part 3, "Canning Food Basics," for complete instructions.

Because jams, jellies, and preserves are normally processed for less than 10 minutes, wash and sterilize jars by boiling them in a canner for 10 minutes.

2. Prepare jars, lids, and canner
Prepare your jars, lids, and canner as outlined in Part 3, "Canning Food Basics." Keep jars and lids on simmer until ready to use.

1. Wash fruit

Wash fruit in plenty of cold, running water. Discard any that are overripe or spoiled, and remove stems if necessary. Do not peel, seed, or core before extracting juice.

2. Heat fruit

Heat fruit as directed in the recipe. Use a potato masher to gently crush soft fruit, and then warm gently over low heat until soft, about 5 to 10 minutes. Cut up and heat firmer fruit with a small amount of water to get the juices flowing, about 20 to 25 minutes.

3. Extract juice

Put warmed fruit in a damp jelly bag with a stand, and set over a large bowl. Allow to drain undisturbed for several hours.

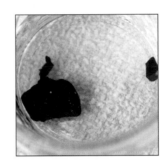

4. Test pectin levels

See "All About Pectin" for more information.

Use the alcohol method or cooking test to ensure fruit has enough pectin to gel. If pectin levels are too low, use one of the low-pectin recipes in this book. If pectin levels are adequate, proceed to cooking.

Guidelines for Extracting Juice*

Fruit	Cups of Water to Add per Pound (per Gram)	Minutes to Simmer Before Juice Extraction
Apples	1 (453.5)	20–25
Blackberries	0–¼ (0–113.5)	5–10
Concord Grapes	0–¼ (0–113.5)	5–10
Crabapples	1 (453.5)	20–25
Plums	½ (226.75)	15–20

The quantities of water provided are for jelly made without pectin. When using commercial pectin, it may be necessary to use more water. Refer to the recipes in this book or the recipe insert provided in your pectin package.

Tartrate Crystals

When extracting juice for grape jelly, it's necessary to allow the juice to stand overnight to prevent the formation of tartrate crystals, which are small, sharp crystals that form due to the high concentration of tartaric acid in grape juice. While these crystals are harmless, they add an unpleasant, crunchy texture and can ruin an otherwise lovely jelly. After extracting juice, cover and rest it in the refrigerator overnight. Sediment will fall to the bottom. Carefully pour the clear juice through a double thickness of cheesecloth, taking care to leave all of the sediment behind, and proceed with your recipe.

5. Mix juice and sugar

Measure the amount of juice called for in your recipe into a large saucepan. Add sugar, and stir to combine well.

6. Bring to a boil

Bring juice and sugar mixture to a boil over high heat. For best results, attach a candy thermometer to the side of the saucepan, ensuring it does not touch the bottom.

7. Cook to 8 degrees above boiling point

If you are not using a thermometer, see "Testing Gel Stages."
If you live at an elevation up to 1,000 feet (305 m) above sea level, cook jelly to exactly 220°F (104°C) as registered on a candy thermometer. If you live more than 1,000 feet (305 m) above sea level, see "Testing Gel Stages" for altitude-adjustment instructions.

8. Fill jars

Using a jar funnel, pour jelly into hot, sterilized canning jars, leaving 1/4 inch (.75 cm) headspace.

9. Remove bubbles and check headspace
Stir jelly gently with a bubble remover to remove bubbles that formed during the boiling process. Using the opposite end of the bubble remover, check headspace on each jar. Add or remove liquid if necessary.

10. Clean jar rims and affix lids
Use a clean kitchen towel and hot water to wipe the edge of each jar, removing every speck of food and syrup. Place a hot lid on each jar, and screw bands to fingertip tightness.

11. Place jars in canner
Place filled jars in the canning rack, and gently submerge them in the simmering water. Put the lid on the pot, and turn heat to the highest setting.

12. Process jars
When water has come to a boil and steam begins to escape from the lid, set a timer for the amount of time specified in the recipe. After that time, turn off the heat, and leave jars in the canner for 5 minutes.

13. Remove jars, check, and store
Remove jars carefully, and set on a heatproof surface lined with kitchen towels for 24 hours. Wipe jars clean or rinse under room-temperature running water. Check seals carefully, and store for up to 2 years.

Preparing Jellies

Concord Grape Jelly (No Pectin)

This can be one of those recipes that's more expensive to make than buy. However, one taste of a sparkling, tender spoonful of this will convince you it's okay to splurge sometimes.

Yield: About 2 to 4 half-pints

3½ lb. (1.5 kg) Concord grapes (to yield 4 cups juice)

¼ cup water (optional)

3 cups granulated sugar

1. Place grapes in a large pot, and use a potato masher to crush. If necessary, add water to prevent grapes from scorching. Heat over medium heat until softened, stirring frequently, about 10 minutes.

2. Carefully transfer grapes to a jelly bag set over a large bowl or a strainer lined with several layers of cheesecloth, and let stand until juice is extracted, which can take 2 to 3 hours. Refrigerate juice overnight.

3. Strain juice through a strainer lined with several layers of cheesecloth.

4. Stir juice and sugar in a large, heavy-bottomed pot over medium-high heat to dissolve. Attach a candy thermometer to the side of the pot, ensuring it does not touch the bottom.

5. Bring mixture to a boil over high heat, and cook until the temperature reaches the gel point of 220°F (104°C) or jelly passes the refrigerator or sheeting test (see "Testing Pectin Levels").

6. Using a canning funnel, ladle jelly into hot, sterilized, half-pint jars, leaving ¼ inch (.75 cm) headspace. Use a bubble remover to remove air pockets, and adjust headspace if necessary. Wipe jar rims and affix two-piece lids.

7. Process for 5 minutes in a boiling-water canner. At the end of the processing time, turn off the heat and let the canner stand, uncovered, for 5 minutes.

8. Remove jars to cooling racks or several layers of kitchen towels, and cool for 24 hours before checking seals and storing.

Tart Cherry-Apple Jelly (with Pectin)

You can make a beautiful cherry-apple jelly with juice, sugar, and liquid pectin. If you have access to freshly pressed juice, you'll achieve the best results.

Yield: About 6 half-pints

- 2 cups tart cherry juice
- 2 cups apple juice
- 6 cups granulated sugar
- 2 pkg. liquid pectin

1. Stir cherry juice, apple juice, and sugar in a large, heavy-bottomed pot over medium-high heat until sugar has dissolved.

2. Bring to a boil over high heat, and cook for 3 minutes. Remove from heat, stir in liquid pectin, and return to high heat for 3 minutes, stirring gently and continuously.

3. Using a canning funnel, ladle jelly into hot, sterilized half-pint jars, leaving 1/4 inch (.75 cm) headspace. Use a bubble remover to remove air pockets, and adjust headspace if necessary. Wipe jar rims and affix two-piece lids.

4. Process for 5 minutes in a boiling-water canner. At the end of the processing time, turn off the heat and let the canner stand, uncovered, for 5 minutes.

5. Remove jars to cooling racks or several layers of kitchen towels, and cool for 24 hours before checking seals and storing.

Variation: Use 4 cups bottled cranberry juice for a sparkling-clear *Cranberry Jelly*, or 4 cups freshly pressed apple cider for *Apple Cider Jelly*.

Helpful Hint

When using liquid pectin, open the packets before you begin, and place them in a measuring cup or coffee mug. They'll be ready when you are.

Making Fruit Butter

Fruit butters are smooth, delicious, and easy to make. The only thing you need is patience, as you'll need to stir the mixture until the fruit cooks down into a thick, luscious spread.

What You'll Need

Jars	Sugar
Lids and seals	Spices (if using)
Canner	Spoon
Fruit	Jar funnel
Paring knife	Kitchen towels
Pots	Bubble remover
Food mill or sieve	

Before You Begin

1. Sterilize canning jars
See Part 3, "Canning Food Basics," for complete instructions.

As fruit butters are normally processed for less than 10 minutes, wash and sterilize jars by boiling in a canner for 10 minutes.

2. Prepare jars, lids, and canner
Prepare your jars, lids, and canner as outlined in Part 3, "Canning Food Basics." Keep jars and lids on simmer until ready to use.

1. Wash
Wash fruit in plenty of cold, running water.

2. Trim
Check fruit for soft spots or blemishes, and trim away. Reserve very soft or overripe fruit for immediate consumption.

3. Cut
Slice fruit as directed in recipe. Remove stems and pits if necessary. Do not peel. Do not discard apple cores or peel apples; they contain a large amount of pectin—just cook them down with the fruit.

4. Heat fruit and liquids
Gently stir together fruit and liquids in a large pot, and cook slowly until fruit is soft, about 30 minutes.

Making Fruit Butter

Apple Butter

Apple butter is so easy to make, and it smells amazing on the stove! Everyone you know will want a jar.

Yield: About 6 half-pints

4 lb. (1.75 kg) apples, sliced, peels and cores intact

1 cup apple cider

1 cup apple cider vinegar

1 cup plus 2 TB. granulated sugar

1 cup plus 2 TB. lightly packed brown sugar

2 TB. ground cinnamon

1 tsp. ground cloves

1. Place apples, apple cider, and apple cider vinegar in a large, heavy-bottomed pot over medium heat. Cook, stirring occasionally, until apples are soft, about 20 minutes. Run apples through a food mill to remove cores, seeds, and peels.

2. Return apple purée to pot with granulated sugar, brown sugar, cinnamon, and cloves. Cook over medium heat until mixture is thick and apple butter mounds on a spoon with no runny liquid around the edges, about 20 minutes.

3. Using a canning funnel, ladle jam into prepared half-pint jars, leaving $1/4$ inch (.75 cm) headspace. Use a bubble remover to remove air pockets, and adjust headspace if necessary. Wipe jar rims and affix two-piece lids.

4. Process for 10 minutes in a boiling-water canner. At the end of the processing time, turn off the heat and let the canner stand, uncovered, for 5 minutes.

5. Remove jars to cooling racks or several layers of kitchen towels, and cool for 24 hours before checking seals and storing.

Pear Butter

This pear butter is simple and not too sweet. Try it spooned into oatmeal, over waffles, or spread on toast.

Yield: About 4 pints

5 lb. (2.25 kg) pears, peeled, sliced, cores intact

1 cup water

2 cups granulated sugar

For Safety's Sake

Canning your own pumpkin or winter squash butter is a no-no! Neither the USDA nor the National Center for Home Food Preservation offers approved methods for canning pumpkin and winter squash butters at home, as the viscosity of winter squashes makes heat penetration unpredictable. Avoid home-canned pumpkin and squash butters. If you must have it, purchase a commercially prepared product, cook it fresh and refrigerate for up to 2 weeks, or freeze for longer storage.

1. Place pears and water in a large, heavy-bottomed pot over medium heat. Cook, stirring occasionally, until pears are soft, about 20 minutes. Run pears through a food mill to remove cores and seeds.

2. Return pear purée to the pot with granulated sugar, and cook over medium heat until the mixture is thick and pear butter mounds on a spoon with no runny liquid around the edges, about 20 minutes.

3. Using a canning funnel, ladle pear butter into prepared half-pint jars, leaving $1/4$ inch (.75 cm) headspace. Use a bubble remover to remove air pockets, and adjust headspace if necessary. Wipe jar rims and affix two-piece lids.

4. Process for 10 minutes in a boiling-water canner. At the end of the processing time, turn off the heat and let the canner stand, uncovered, for 5 minutes.

5. Remove jars to cooling racks or several layers of kitchen towels, and cool for 24 hours before checking seals and storing.

Canning Tomatoes and Tomato Products

Tomatoes are the most commonly canned food in the United States. If you grow them in your garden, you know how quickly the harvest can get out of hand. Canning helps to preserve the bounty, so you can enjoy it all year long. Tomatoes can be canned whole, halved, or crushed. Salsa, ketchup, barbecue sauce, and tomato jam complete your tomato pantry, and provide a delightful taste of summer all year round.

Tomato Canning Basics

Choose firm, ripe, and unblemished tomatoes for canning. Paste or plum varieties are best for home canning, due to their high acidity, low water content, and meaty texture.

Spoiler Alert!

Tomatoes are widely considered a high-acid food (their pH values are below 4.6), but many factors—including spoilage and overripening—can bring the pH level above 4.6. If tomatoes are overripe, split, blemished, or cracked, don't can them. And do not can tomatoes from vines that are dead, decayed, or frost-killed. Cherry and grape tomatoes have a lower acid content and should never be canned, so save these varieties to be eaten fresh, or cook and freeze them immediately.

The most common causes of spoilage in home-canned tomatoes are underprocessing and poor seals. Review Part 3, "Canning Food Basics," before you proceed with your tomato canning project. Follow instructions carefully, and be sure to process jars for the recommended amount of time.

Cans of tomatoes that have failed to seal can be reprocessed within 24 hours. If a jar loses its seal after a few days, it is an indication of spoilage, and the tomatoes should be discarded. See Part 3, "Canning Food Basics," for more information on troubleshooting and disposal of spoiled food.

Safe Processing

To ensure safe pH levels, home-canned tomatoes must be acidified. Add 2 tablespoons bottled lemon juice or 1/2 teaspoon citric acid to each quart (halve these amounts when canning pints).

If you prefer not to acidify your tomatoes, refer to Part 8, "Pressure Canning."

Follow the Recipe

The recipes in this book were written following USDA standards and have been pH tested for safety. Many home canners add foods, such as fresh herbs or peppers, to home-canned tomato recipes. This alters the pH level of the recipe and can lead to the growth of botulism and other dangerous spoilers. Follow each recipe exactly as written.

Nutrient Rich Year Round

The flavor of home-canned tomatoes is superior to store-bought. In addition, when heat is added to tomatoes during the canning process, it makes the lycopene (a powerful antioxidant) more powerful, so canned tomatoes are healthy, too!

Lemon Juice

Always use bottled lemon juice when canning tomatoes, as it is guaranteed to have an acidity level of 5 percent. Fresh lemon juice is not an acceptable substitute.

Troubleshooting Canned Tomatoes

Problem: Tomatoes float in the jar.

Solutions: Use the hot-pack method. Pack jars as firmly as possible without crushing tomatoes, and be sure to press all air bubbles out of the jar before sealing. Use regular-mouth jars, rather than wide-mouth jars, so the shoulders of the jar hold the tomatoes down. Floating tomatoes are unsightly, but they're still safe to eat.

Problem: Liquids and solids separate.

Solutions: Some separation of liquids and solids will occur when tomatoes are allowed to heat, then cool, and are heated again. Use the hot-pack method when canning whole tomatoes, or use the "batch" method of heating tomatoes described in both the Tomato Juice and Tomato Sauce recipes in this part. If your sauce separates, it's still okay to use it.

Storing jars without screw bands allows you to easily detect signs of spoilage and prevents mold or moisture from ruining your canned goods.

Problem: Black spots on the lid of the jar.

Solutions: This is usually caused by food adhering to the jar lid during processing. If no other signs of spoilage are present, the tomatoes are still safe to eat.

Canning Whole Tomatoes

Choose perfectly ripe, unblemished plum, paste, or Roma tomatoes, and put them up as soon as you can, preferably within 24 hours of harvest. You will need about 22 to 24 pounds (10 to 10.75 kg) raw tomatoes for 7 quarts, and about 11 to 14 pounds (5 to 6.25 kg) for 7 pints.

For shorter processing times, consider using a pressure canner (see Part 8, "Pressure Canning").

What You'll Need

Tomatoes

Canning jars and rings

New canning seals

Boiling-water canner

Paring knife

Pot or blancher

Ice bath

Bottled lemon juice or citric acid

Salt (optional)

Stock pot

Water or homemade tomato juice

Canning funnel

Ladle

Bubble remover

Cooling racks or kitchen towels

Before You Begin

1. Wash
Wash tomatoes carefully under cold, running water.

2. Prepare jars, lids, and canner
Prepare jars, lids, and canner as outlined in Part 3, "Canning Food Basics." Keep jars and lids on simmer until ready to use.

1. Blanch
Cut an x in the bottom (blossom end) of each tomato. Blanch in boiling water for 1 minute, and transfer to an ice bath.

2. Peel
Remove the core of each tomato, and peel off the skin. Halve if desired, or leave whole.

3. Add acid and salt
Add 2 tablespoons bottled lemon juice or $1/2$ teaspoon citric acid to each hot, sterilized quart jar (halve this amount for pints). If desired, add 1 teaspoon salt per quart ($1/2$ teaspoon per pint).

Raw-Packing Tomatoes

Raw-packed tomatoes are much more likely to separate during the canning process, and require longer processing times. It's worthwhile to take the extra time and use the hot-pack method.

If you wish to raw-pack, use the following instructions: Pack tomatoes loosely into hot, prepared jars and cover with boiling water, leaving ½ inch (2.5 cm) headspace. Use a bubble remover to remove as much air as possible, and adjust headspace if necessary.

4. Pack
For hot pack (recommended), place tomatoes in a large stock pot with water or tomato juice to cover. Bring to a boil, and cook for 5 minutes. Using a canning funnel and a ladle, pack tomatoes loosely in jars and cover with hot liquid, leaving ½ inch (1.25 cm) headspace. Use a bubble remover to gently remove as much air as possible, and adjust headspace if necessary.

5. Seal
Carefully wipe jar rims, adjust lids, and screw bands as tightly as you can with your fingertips without using additional force.

6. Process
See the "Processing Times for Canned Whole Tomatoes" table.

Process tomatoes in a boiling-water canner according to the table with 2 inches (5 cm) water to cover, setting the timer as soon as the water comes to a full boil.

7. Cool
Uncover the canner, and let jars stand for 5 minutes. Remove to cooling racks or several layers of kitchen towels, and let stand, undisturbed, for 24 hours. Check seals, and store for up to 1 year.

Processing Times for Canned Whole Tomatoes

Product	Pack Method	Processing Time*
Tomatoes, whole or halved, in water	Hot or raw pack	Pints: 40 minutes Quarts: 45 minutes
Tomatoes, whole or halved, in homemade juice	Hot pack	Pints or quarts: 90 minutes

*Refer to Part 3, "Canning Food Basics" for altitude adjustment charts if you are more than 1,001 feet (300 m) above sea level. Your local government service organization or agricultural extension can tell you your altitude if you are unsure.

Water Levels

As with all boiling-water canning projects, it's important to ensure that jars are covered with boiling water by 2 inches (5 cm) throughout the processing time. During longer processing times, such as those required for quarts of tomatoes or tomatoes packed in juice, keep a large kettle of hot water at the ready. If necessary, add boiling water during the processing time to ensure jars are covered by 2 inches (5 cm). And be sure to add boiling water—if you lose your boil, you'll have to start the processing time over again!

Part 6: Canning Tomatoes and Tomato Products

Tomato Juice

Canned homemade tomato juice makes a delicious beverage, as well as a terrific base for vegetable soups.

Yield: About 7 pints

14 lb. (6.25 kg) ripe, juicy tomatoes

7 TB. bottled lemon juice or 1¾ tsp. citric acid

3½ tsp. kosher salt (optional)

1. Quickly cut 1 pound (453.5 g) tomatoes into quarters, and place in a large pot. Using a potato masher, mash tomatoes, and stir over high heat while bringing mixture to a boil.

2. Continue to cut and add tomatoes to boiling tomato mixture in the same-size batches, returning mixture to a boil before each addition.

3. Once all tomatoes have been added, cook for about 10 minutes, stirring frequently, until tomatoes are soft.

4. Run cooked tomatoes through a food mill or sieve to remove skin and seeds.

5. Add 1 tablespoon bottled lemon juice or ¼ teaspoon citric acid to each hot, clean pint jar. Add ½ teaspoon kosher salt to each jar (if using).

6. Return tomato juice to a boil, and use a canning funnel to fill jars, leaving ½ inch (1.25 cm) headspace. Use a bubble remover to remove air pockets, and adjust headspace if necessary. Affix two-piece canning lids, and screw bands to fingertip tightness.

7. Process jars in a boiling-water canner with water to cover by 2 inches (5 cm) for 40 minutes. At the end of the processing time, turn off the heat and let the canner stand, uncovered, for 5 minutes.

8. Remove jars to cooling racks or several layers of kitchen towels, and cool for 24 hours before checking seals and storing.

Variation: For *Tomato-Vegetable Juice,* once all tomatoes have been added to the large pot, add ¼ cup each finely diced carrots, celery, onion, and bell pepper, and simmer for 20 minutes. Proceed with the rest of the tomato juice recipe.

Canning Caution

Don't can tomatoes in commercially prepared juice. Commercial tomato juices are thicker than homemade juices, and their "tinny" flavor can be unpleasant.

Tomato Sauce

Cutting tomatoes releases enzymes that separate liquids from solids. Cutting, cooking, and crushing them 1 pound (453.5 g) or less at a time quickly destroys these enzymes, producing a perfect, smooth purée of tomato sauce.

Yield: About 7 quarts

22 to 24 lb. (10 to 10.75 kg) plum, paste, or Roma tomatoes

14 TB. bottled lemon juice or 3½ tsp. citric acid

7 tsp. kosher salt (optional)

Don't Use Garlic or Basil

Resist the urge to add garlic or basil to your home-canned tomatoes. Even this small addition can change the pH level of your finished product, making it unsafe.

1. Quickly cut 1 pound (453.5 g) tomatoes into quarters, and place in a large pot. Using a potato masher, mash tomatoes, and stir over high heat while bringing mixture to a boil.

2. Continue to cut and add tomatoes to boiling tomato mixture in the same-size batches, returning mixture to a boil before each addition. Continue to crush each batch of tomatoes with the potato masher.

3. Once all tomatoes have been added, continue to cook over medium heat for 5 minutes.

4. Run cooked tomatoes through a food mill or sieve to remove skin and seeds.

5. Return tomato sauce to the stock pot, and simmer, stirring often, until reduced by one third for thin sauce and by one half for a thicker sauce, about 20 to 30 minutes.

6. Add 1 tablespoon bottled lemon juice or ¼ teaspoon citric acid to each hot, clean pint jar. Add ½ teaspoon kosher salt to each jar (if using).

7. Fill hot jars with sauce, leaving ½ inch (1.25 cm) headspace. Use a bubble remover to remove air pockets, and adjust headspace if necessary. Adjust two-piece lids, and tighten bands to fingertip tightness.

8. Process jars in a boiling-water canner with water to cover by 2 inches (5 cm) for 50 minutes. At the end of the processing time, turn off the heat and let the canner stand, uncovered, for 5 minutes.

9. Remove jars to cooling racks or several layers of kitchen towels, and cool for 24 hours before checking seals and storing.

Making Salsa

You can process salsa in a boiling-water canner if you follow the instructions carefully. Both ripe and green tomatoes make great salsa. While spices are optional when canning salsas, be sure to keep the vegetable ratios as written in the recipes, and follow the processing times to the letter.

What You'll Need

Tomatoes	Peppers
Canning jars and rings	Onions
New canning seals	Canning funnel
Boiling-water canner	Ladle
Paring knife	Bubble remover
Pot or blancher	Cooling racks or kitchen towels
Ice bath	

Before You Begin

1. Wash
Wash tomatoes carefully under cold, running water.

2. Prepare jars, lids, and canner
Prepare your jars, lids, and canner as outlined in Part 3, "Canning Food Basics." Keep the jars and lids on simmer until ready to use.

1. Blanch
Cut an x in the bottom (blossom end) of each tomato. Blanch in boiling water for 1 minute, and transfer to an ice bath.

2. Peel
Remove the core of each tomato, and peel off the skin.

3. Chop and cook
Measure tomatoes, peppers, and onions precisely, and chop in uniform pieces as the recipe directs. Prepare salsa as directed in the recipe.

4. Pack
Use a canning funnel and ladle to pack salsas in hot canning jars. Use a bubble remover to remove air pockets, and adjust headspace if necessary per recipe.

5. Seal
Wipe rims, adjust two-piece lids, and screw bands to fingertip tightness.

6. Process and cool
Process salsa in a boiling-water canner with 2 inches (5 cm) water to cover for recipe time. Uncover the canner, and let jars stand for 5 minutes. Remove to cooling racks or kitchen towels, and let stand for 24 hours. Check seals, and store for up to 1 year.

Salsa Safety

- Salsa is considered a low-acid food; therefore, it needs to be acidified before processing in a boiling-water canner to ensure safety. It's not safe to can your favorite, untested salsa recipe. If you have a recipe you love, freeze it instead.

- While it is safe to substitute bottled lemon juice for vinegar in salsa recipes, it is not safe to substitute vinegar for lemon juice, as the pH of the finished product may be unsafe.

- You may adjust the seasonings slightly, but the ratio of vegetables must remain the same.

- Homemade salsas can seem watery, but adding thickeners (such as cornstarch) changes both the viscosity and pH of the finished product, making an unsafe canned salsa. If you want a thicker salsa, pour off some of the liquid after you open the jar, or use thickeners just before serving—never before canning!

- Hot peppers can burn your skin, so wear gloves, and handle them carefully. Removing the seeds and white membrane (pith) from hot peppers will substantially reduce their fiery flavor.

- Fill jars to exactly ½ inch (1.25 cm) headspace. If you have a jar that isn't quite full, don't process it; refrigerate it and eat it within 2 weeks.

Plum Tomato Salsa

Plum or paste tomatoes make a thicker, more flavorful salsa than slicing tomatoes. This recipe makes a mild, tasty salsa.

Yield: About 6 to 8 pints

10 cups peeled and diced plum tomatoes

3 cups seeded and diced red bell peppers

2 1/2 cups finely chopped Hungarian wax peppers

1/2 cup finely chopped hot chile peppers (such as jalapeño or Anaheim)

4 cups diced onion

1 cup apple cider vinegar (5 percent acidity)

3 tsp. kosher salt

1 tsp. oregano leaves

2 TB. granulated sugar (optional)

12 to 16 TB. bottled lemon juice

1. Place plum tomatoes, red bell peppers, Hungarian wax peppers, hot chile peppers, onion, apple cider vinegar, kosher salt, oregano, and sugar (if using) in a medium saucepan. Bring to a boil over medium-high heat, and cook for 30 minutes.

2. Add 2 tablespoons bottled lemon juice to each hot pint jar. Using a jar funnel, fill each jar with salsa to 1/2 inch (1.25 cm) headspace, and stir gently to distribute lemon juice. Use a bubble remover to remove air pockets, and adjust headspace if necessary. Wipe jar rims, affix two-piece lids, and screw bands to fingertip tightness.

3. Process jars in a boiling-water canner with water to cover by 2 inches (5 cm) for 15 minutes. At the end of the processing time, turn off the heat and let the canner stand, uncovered, for 5 minutes.

4. Remove jars to cooling racks or several layers of kitchen towels, and cool for 24 hours before checking seals and storing.

Variations: For *Chipotle Salsa,* reduce the quantity of hot chile peppers to 2 tablespoons and add 2 tablespoons chopped, canned chipotle chiles or rehydrated, chopped dried chipotle chiles.

For *Medium Salsa,* reduce red bell peppers to 2 1/2 cups, increase hot chile peppers to 1 cup, and add 2 tablespoons ground cumin.

For *Hot Salsa,* eliminate red bell peppers and add 2 tablespoons ground cumin. Use 6 cups mixed chiles—a mix of mild and hot chile peppers—to make it as hot as you like. Try blending Anaheim, poblano, jalapeño, and Hungarian wax peppers and adding a habanero or Serrano chile or two if you dare. Just make sure that you add exactly 6 cups of peppers to keep the recipe safe for canning.

Canned Whole Tomatillos

Unlike tomatoes, tomatillos do not need to be peeled—simply remove the papery husks, wash, cut if needed, and can them! Look for firm, deep-green fruit in a green husk for best quality.

Yield: About 7 quarts

14 lb. (10 kg) fresh tomatillos

14 TB. bottled lemon juice or 3$\frac{1}{2}$ tsp. citric acid

7 tsp. kosher salt (optional)

1. Husk tomatillos and wash well. Tomatillos have a sticky surface beneath the husk, so you may wish to wear gloves.

2. Using the hot-pack method, place tomatillos in a stock pot with enough water just to cover. Bring to a boil, and cook for 10 minutes.

3. Add 2 tablespoons bottled lemon juice or $\frac{1}{2}$ teaspoon citric acid to each hot, prepared quart jar. Drain tomatillos, and pack into jars. Cover with fresh boiling water, leaving $\frac{1}{2}$ inch (1.25 cm) headspace. Use a bubble remover to remove air pockets, and adjust headspace if necessary. Wipe rims, adjust lids, and screw bands to fingertip tightness.

4. Process tomatillos in a boiling-water canner with 2 inches (5 cm) water to cover for 45 minutes for quarts and 40 minutes for pints. Uncover the canner, and let jars stand for 5 minutes.

5. Remove to cooling racks or several layers of kitchen towels, and let stand, undisturbed, for 24 hours. Check seals, and store for up to 1 year.

Variation: Use this method to can unripe green tomatoes.

Hot Salsa Verde

Fiery chile peppers and tomatillos make a delicious enchilada sauce or tortilla chip dip!

Yield: About 4 pints

2 lb. ('907.25 g) fresh tomatillos

2 cups finely chopped jalapeño peppers

4 cups finely chopped sweet onion

1 cup bottled lemon juice

2 TB. finely chopped fresh cilantro

1 tsp. dried oregano

1 TB. canning salt

1. Husk tomatillos and wash well.

2. Place tomatillos, jalapeño peppers, sweet onion, bottled lemon juice, cilantro, oregano, and canning salt in a large saucepan, and bring to a boil over medium-high heat. Cook for 10 minutes.

3. Ladle salsa into hot, prepared jars, leaving ¹/₂ inch (1.25 cm) headspace. Use a bubble remover to remove air pockets, and adjust headspace if necessary. Wipe rims, adjust lids, and screw bands to fingertip tightness.

4. Process in a boiling-water canner for 15 minutes. Uncover the canner, and let jars stand for 5 minutes.

5. Remove to cooling racks or several layers of kitchen towels, and let stand, undisturbed, for 24 hours. Check seals, and store for up to 1 year.

Part 6: Canning Tomatoes and Tomato Products

Ketchup

You'll never want bottled ketchup again after you taste this sweet, spicy, and tangy condiment!

Yield: About 6 to 7 pints

24 lb. (11 kg) peeled and diced plum tomatoes

3 cups finely chopped onion

2 tsp. cayenne pepper

½ tsp. ground nutmeg

3 cups apple cider vinegar (5 percent acidity)

4 tsp. whole cloves

3 cinnamon sticks, lightly crushed

1½ tsp. allspice berries

4 sprigs fresh thyme

2 TB. celery seeds

1 tsp. whole cumin seeds

1½ cups granulated sugar

¼ cup kosher salt

1. Put plum tomatoes, onion, cayenne pepper, and nutmeg in a large stock pot, and bring to a boil over medium-high heat. Reduce heat to medium-low, and cook for 20 minutes, stirring often.

2. Put apple cider vinegar in a saucepan. Cut a square of cheesecloth to make a spice bag, and add cloves, cinnamon sticks, allspice berries, thyme, celery seeds, and cumin seeds. Add the spice bag to the saucepan, and bring to a boil over high heat. Turn off heat, and steep for 20 minutes.

3. Remove spice bag from vinegar, and pour vinegar into tomato mixture. Return to a boil, and cook over medium heat for 30 minutes.

4. Press tomato mixture through a food mill or sieve to remove any seeds. Return to the stock pot, and add sugar and kosher salt. Bring to a boil and cook over medium-high heat, stirring almost constantly, until mixture is reduced by half and liquid does not separate when mounded on a spoon.

5. Using a jar funnel, ladle ketchup into hot pint jars, leaving ¼ inch (.5 cm) headspace. Use a bubble remover to remove air pockets, and adjust headspace if necessary. Wipe jar rims, affix two-piece lids, and screw bands to fingertip tightness.

6. Process jars in a boiling-water canner with 2 inches (5 cm) water to cover for 15 minutes. Turn off the heat, and let the canner stand, uncovered, for 5 minutes.

7. Remove jars to cooling racks or several layers of kitchen towels, and cool for 24 hours before checking seals and storing.

Barbecue Sauce

Bottled, store-bought sauce can't compare to the flavor of this rich and spicy barbecue sauce. Plan to give a jar to everyone who tastes it!

Yield: About 6 to 8 half-pints

20 cups peeled and diced plum tomatoes

1½ cups finely chopped onion

½ cup finely chopped red or green bell peppers

1 TB. cayenne pepper

1 TB. ground nutmeg

1 TB. celery seeds

1½ cups lightly packed dark brown sugar

1 cup apple cider vinegar (5 percent acidity)

⅓ cup bottled lemon juice

2 TB. soy sauce

1 TB. + 1 tsp. ground ginger

1 tsp. oregano leaves

½ tsp. ground cinnamon

½ tsp. ground cloves

1. Place plum tomatoes, onion, red or green bell peppers, cayenne pepper, and nutmeg in a large saucepan. Bring to a boil over medium-high heat, stirring constantly. Reduce heat to medium-low, and cook for 30 minutes.

2. Press tomato mixture through a food mill or sieve to purée and remove any seeds.

3. Return mixture to the saucepan, and stir in celery seeds, dark brown sugar, apple cider vinegar, bottled lemon juice, soy sauce, ginger, oregano, cinnamon, and cloves. Bring to a boil, stirring constantly. Cook over medium-high heat, stirring frequently, until mixture resembles the consistency of loose ketchup, about 30 minutes.

4. Using a jar funnel, ladle sauce into hot half-pint jars, leaving ¼ inch (.5 cm) headspace. Use a bubble remover to remove any pockets of air, and adjust headspace if necessary. Wipe jar rims, affix two-piece lids, and screw bands to fingertip tightness.

5. Process in a boiling-water canner with 2 inches (5 cm) water to cover for 15 minutes. Turn off the heat, and let the canner stand, uncovered, for 5 minutes.

6. Remove jars to cooling racks or several layers of kitchen towels, and cool for 24 hours before checking seals and storing.

Barbecue Sauce

Tomato Jam

This sweet and spicy tomato jam is a great accompaniment to breakfast or brunch foods, fish, or chicken, and can also be used as a unique bagel spread or burger condiment.

Yield: About 4 half-pints

5 lb. (2.25 kg) unpeeled and diced plum tomatoes

$3^{1}/_{2}$ cups granulated sugar

$^{1}/_{2}$ cup bottled lemon juice

2 garlic cloves, finely chopped

1 TB. grated fresh ginger

1 TB. crushed red pepper flakes

1 TB. kosher salt

$^{1}/_{2}$ tsp. ground cinnamon

$^{1}/_{2}$ tsp. ground cumin

$^{1}/_{2}$ tsp. ground cloves

1. Place plum tomatoes, sugar, bottled lemon juice, garlic, ginger, crushed red pepper flakes, kosher salt, cinnamon, cumin, and cloves in a stock pot. Bring to a boil over medium-high heat, stirring constantly. Reduce heat to medium-low, and cook, stirring frequently, until mixture is thick and "jammy," about 1 hour.

2. Using a canning funnel, ladle tomato jam into hot half-pint jars, leaving $^{1}/_{4}$ inch (.5 cm) headspace. Use a bubble remover to remove any air pockets, and adjust headspace if necessary. Wipe jar rims, affix two-piece lids, and screw bands to fingertip tightness.

3. Process jars in a boiling-water canner for 20 minutes. Turn off the heat, and let the canner stand, uncovered, for 5 minutes.

4. Remove jars to cooling racks or several layers of kitchen towels, and cool for 24 hours before checking seals and storing.

Green Tomato Marmalade

Green tomatoes, ginger, and a hint of yuzu (an Asian citrus fruit similar to grapefruit) combine for a fun, Asian-inspired marmalade. If you can't find yuzu, grapefruit will work just as well.

Yield: About 3 to 4 half-pints

2 lb. (907.25 g) seeded and finely chopped green tomatoes

2 TB. yuzu or grapefruit zest

2 TB. freshly grated ginger

2½ cups granulated sugar

2 TB. freshly squeezed yuzu or grapefruit juice

2 TB. bottled lemon juice

1 pkt. liquid pectin

1. Place green tomatoes, yuzu or grapefruit zest, ginger, sugar, yuzu or grapefruit juice, and bottled lemon juice in a stock pot. Bring to a boil over high heat, stirring constantly. Reduce heat to medium-low, and cook, stirring frequently, for 10 minutes. Remove from heat, and stir in pectin.

2. Using a canning funnel, ladle marmalade into hot half-pint jars, leaving ¼ inch (.5 cm) headspace. Use a bubble remover to remove air pockets, and adjust headspace if necessary. Wipe jar rims, affix two-piece lids, and screw bands to fingertip tightness.

3. Process jars in a boiling-water canner for 20 minutes. Turn off the heat, and let the canner stand, uncovered, for 5 minutes.

4. Remove jars to cooling racks or several layers of kitchen towels, and cool for 24 hours before checking seals and storing.

Part 7

Pickling

An assortment of pickled fruits and vegetables, cucumber pickles, chutneys, sauerkraut, and relishes bring flavor to the table and add zest and interest to meals. Fermented pickles, such as kosher dills, sauerkraut, and kimchi, also offer health benefits in the form of probiotics—healthy bacteria that enhance digestive and immune system function. It's easy to make your own pickles at home, and the results are far superior to anything that you can buy in a store.

Tools and Equipment for Pickling

Most of the equipment you'll need for pickling is standard home-canning equipment, which I discussed in Part 3, "Canning Food Basics"; however, I'll give you a quick overview of the equipment just in case. The only extra investment you'll need to make is in large jars with lids for making fermented pickles.

Pickling crocks

To ferment pickles, you need a large vessel with a wide mouth. Stoneware crocks are traditionally used for this purpose, but I'm partial to large glass jars with lids, which allow me to see foods as they are fermenting. Check crocks before use to be sure that there are no cracks or chips on the interior. If you shop for flea market stoneware finds, you'll also want to make sure the crocks are glazed on the inside as well as the outside and don't contain harmful substances, such as lead or cadmium. New crocks are the safest choice.

Boiling-water canner

A boiling-water canner, or water-bath canner, is made of porcelain-covered steel or aluminum. These large pots with tight-fitting lids and jar racks are used to can high-acid foods, including pickles.

Two-piece lids

Canning lids are comprised of a lid and a screw band. While screw bands can be reused as long as they are not dented or rusted, you must always use new lids for each canning project. Once jars are sealed, remove the screw bands for storage.

Jar funnel

A jar funnel has a wider mouth than regular kitchen funnels, allowing you to quickly and neatly fill jars with hot foods.

Canning jars

Tempered-glass "Mason"-type jars that can be fitted with two-piece lids are the safest choice for home canning. Pickles are most frequently canned in half-pint, pint, and quart jars.

Bubble remover/headspace tool

This inexpensive, multifunction plastic tool removes air pockets from your foods before canning. It also has helpful notches that allow you to check headspace. Leaving the appropriate amount of headspace is essential for safe and successful canning.

Instant-read or candy thermometer

Low temperature processing of pickles requires the use of a candy thermometer to ensure that the water remains at 180°F (82°C) throughout the processing time to ensure safety. Look for an easy-to-read thermometer that clips securely to the side of your pot without touching the bottom, and read all the instructions for it before use.

Lid wand

A lid wand is a heatproof tool with a small magnet at the end. Use it to safely remove hot lids from simmering water without burning your fingers.

Jar lifter

A jar lifter makes it easy to safely remove hot jars from your canner. These heatproof tongs are designed to gently remove jars by the neck without disturbing the bands or seals.

Pickling Basics

Pickling is simply the preservation of fruits or vegetables in a brine made of salt, water, spices, and sometimes vinegar or sugar. Pickling is practiced by nearly every culture throughout the world. Many people think of pickles as just cucumbers in brine, but nearly any fruit or vegetable can be pickled! Pickling once ensured that fruits and vegetables were on the table throughout the long winter months.

Choose firm, freshly harvested cucumbers, fruits, or vegetables. The conventional wisdom for successful pickling is "from vine to brine in 24 hours." Waxy supermarket produce or produce that has been sitting around will yield inferior pickles.

Types of Pickling

Pickles can be made in two ways: by quick pickling, as for fresh-pack pickles, fruit pickles, relishes, and chutneys; and fermented pickling, as for kosher dills, sauerkraut, and kimchi.

If you're a beginner, you'll want to start with a quick pickle. Fresh-pack pickles are quick pickles that are covered in a hot brine and then preserved in a boiling-water canner. Chutneys and relishes are also easy to prepare—chopped fruits or vegetables are cooked in a spicy vinegar solution and canned as you would jam or jelly.

Once you have a little experience under your belt, you can graduate to *fermented* pickles. To ferment pickles, vegetables are prepared in a brine of water and salt, and then fermented at room temperature for a period of several days to several weeks. It's extremely important to understand the practices and pitfalls of fermentation, which occurs under very specific conditions. Follow the instructions in recipes closely, and do not make changes to recipes.

Pickling Spice Recipe

To make a quick and easy mixed pickling spice, combine the following, and store in a tightly sealed jar away from light and heat:

½ cup yellow mustard seeds

¼ cup whole allspice berries

¼ cup mixed peppercorns (black, white, and/or pink)

¼ cup ground mace

¼ cup coriander seeds

6 crushed dry bay leaves

2 TB. crushed red pepper flakes

2 TB. whole cloves

Pickling Ingredients

Some extra ingredients are necessary to pickle foods:

- Spices
- Garlic
- Sugar
- Firming agents (such as Pickle Crisp)
- Pickling or kosher salt
- Vinegar

Be sure these other ingredients are at the peak of freshness. For example, garlic that is immature or old can turn pink or blue in the jar. This is not necessarily dangerous, but it is certainly off-putting in appearance and can affect the flavor as well. The age of your spices makes a difference, too. Choose fresh, whole spices (not powdered), and buy only as much as you can use in one canning season.

Common pickling spices include bay leaf, mustard seed, allspice, coriander, cinnamon, dried chiles, black pepper, cloves, mace, and ginger. If you aren't making huge batches, a commercially prepared mixed pickling spice is a good choice. You can buy it in small bottles at the supermarket, or order 1-pound (453.5-g) packages from online sources.

Your choice of salt is important as well. Use pickling or canning salt for best results. Never use iodized salt, as it contains additives that will darken the pickles and cloud the brine. Kosher salt is an acceptable substitute for canning salt, but remember that it is flaked and measures at twice the volume of canning salt: 1 cup canning salt equals approximately 2 cups kosher salt. However, the most accurate way to substitute is by weight, as 1 cup pure salt weighs 10.2 ounces (289.25 g). For reduced-sodium diets, seek out recipes specifically developed for potassium chloride, as substituting may affect the flavor and quality of the finished product.

Firming agents can be used to make crisp pickles, but use of these products is labor-intensive and sometimes not effective. The calcium in food-grade lime does help to keep pickles crisp, but the process requires soaking, draining, and then resoaking to remove excess lime. Alum is food-safe, but tests have shown no effect on the crispness of the finished pickles. A commercial preparation, such as Pickle Crisp, is a good choice if you want to use a firming agent—it is a granular product made of calcium chloride, and it can be added directly to the jar. Low-temperature processing also helps. For the crunchiest pickles, a soak in ice water is the best solution.

When it comes to vinegar, choose commercial vinegars that have a guaranteed acid level of 5 percent. Never can with homemade vinegar!

Troubleshooting Pickles

Problem: Pickles are shriveled.

Solutions: Choose perfectly fresh produce. Measure all ingredients carefully, as shriveling can be caused by a pickling solution that is too strong. Do not overprocess.

Problem: Pickles are hollow.

Solutions: Hollow pickles usually grew this way or stood at room temperature for too long before processing. You can weed them out by soaking the pickles in water before you begin. The hollow ones will float and should be used for other purposes, such as relish.

Problem: Pickles are discolored.

Solutions: Pickles processed with old garlic or dill can turn odd shades of pink, blue, or purple. This is not a safety issue, merely an aesthetic one. If pickles turn black or are slimy or slippery, they are spoiled and should be discarded.

Problem: White sediment in the jar.

Solutions: When making fermented pickles, white sediment is a normal occurrence. You may notice it in the jar or on the outside of the container if the fermenting liquid bubbles over. In quick-pack pickles, sediment usually occurs when using table salt. In either case, it is not a safety issue.

Avoiding Spoiled Pickled Foods

To avoid spoilage, be sure to remove $1/8$ inch (.25 cm) from the blossom end of your cucumbers, measure brine ingredients carefully, thoroughly wash all produce before you begin, and store finished pickles in a cool, dark location.

You should also use nonreactive utensils when making pickles. Copper cookware and utensils will turn food an odd shade of green, while iron utensils will turn them black. Never use galvanized metal or aluminum utensils or storage containers, as they are treated with cadmium and may produce a toxic substance when they react with the acid and salt in pickled goods.

If your pickles end up soft, slimy, or slippery, they're spoiled. (See Part 3, "Canning Food Basics," for safe disposal methods for spoiled canned goods.)

Follow the Recipe

The recipes in this book were written following USDA standards and have been pH tested for safety. Follow each recipe exactly as written. You may decrease the amount of salt in quick-pack pickles, but never in fermented pickles. You may decrease the amount of dried spice added or substitute one spice for another. Never increase the amount of spice in a recipe or change the amount of fresh herbs, though, as this may affect the pH.

Making Quick-Pack (Fresh-Pack) Pickles

Quick pickles are a fast, easy way to pickle cucumbers, vegetables, and fruits. A quick brine of vinegar with salt, sugar, and spices is all it takes to create tangy, delicious pickles to liven up your meals.

What You'll Need

Treatment solution	Spices
Jars	Filtered or distilled water
Lids and seals	Vinegar
Canner	Sugar
Vegetables or fruit	Pickling or kosher salt
Paring knife	Bubble remover
Ice bath (if needed)	Kitchen towels
Pot or blancher	
Potato peeler	

Before You Begin

1. Prepare treatment solution
See "Preparing Fruits for Canning" for detailed instructions.

If you are making fruit pickles, you will need to prepare a treatment solution. If you're not, skip this step.

2. Prepare jars, lids, and canner
Prepare your jars, lids, and canner as outlined in "Preparing the Jars and Equipment." Keep jars and lids on simmer until ready to use.

1. Wash
Wash vegetables or fruit in plenty of cold, running water.

2. Trim
Check fruit for soft spots or blemishes, and trim away. When canning cucumbers, cut off ⅛ inch (.25 cm) of blossom end. Trim outside skin from watermelon rinds, leaving white parts intact.

3. Soak in ice bath or blanch
If pickling cucumbers, green beans, or carrots, soak in an ice bath for several hours. If pickling fruit such as peaches, blanch in a boiling-water bath, and then dip in an ice bath.

4. Peel and slice
Leave cucumbers unpeeled. Peel unblanched fruit with a potato peeler if called for in the recipe. Slip skins off blanched fruits, and remove pits if necessary.

5. Make pickling solution
Make pickling solution with spices, water, vinegar, sugar, and salt according to the recipe. Bring mixture to a boil, stirring occasionally.

6. Fill jars
Using the raw-pack method, pack raw fruits or vegetables tightly in jars, and then pour boiling pickling liquid into jars, leaving ¹/₂ inch (1.25 cm) headspace.

7. Remove bubbles and check headspace
Run a bubble remover around edges, gently pressing inward so no pockets of air remain. Using the opposite side of the bubble remover, check headspace on each jar. Add or remove liquid if necessary.

8. Clean jar rims and affix lids
Use a clean kitchen towel and hot water to wipe the edge of each jar, removing every speck of food and liquid. Place a hot lid on each jar, and screw bands to fingertip tightness.

9. Place jars in canner
Place filled jars in the canning rack, and gently submerge them in the simmering water. Put the lid on the pot, and turn heat to the highest setting.

10. Process jars
When water has come to a boil and steam begins to escape, set a timer based on the recipe. After that time, turn off the heat, remove the canner lid, and let jars rest in the canner for 5 minutes.

11. Cool and store jars
Remove jars carefully, and set on a heatproof surface lined with kitchen towels for 24 hours. Check seals carefully, and wipe jars clean or rinse under room-temperature running water. Store for up to 2 years.

Quick-Pack Dill Pickles

Chunky cucumbers are packed in a lightly spiced vinegar brine and processed in a boiling-water canner for this fast and easy dill pickle.

Yield: About 4 pints

4 lb. (1.75 kg) pickling (Kirby) cucumbers

1 cup pickling salt

3 qt. filtered water

Ice

1 qt. white vinegar

$1/4$ cup sugar

2 TB. mixed pickling spice

8 tsp. black or yellow mustard seeds

8 TB. dill seed

1. Slice $1/8$ inch (.25 cm) of blossom end off each pickling cucumber, and discard. Slice cucumbers $1\frac{1}{2}$ inches (3.75 cm) thick.

2. In a large bowl, stir $1/2$ cup pickling salt into 2 quarts water until dissolved. Add cucumbers and enough ice to cover, refrigerate, and soak for 1 to 2 hours.

3. Before turning on heat, stir remaining $1/2$ cup pickling salt, remaining 1 quart water, white vinegar, and sugar in a medium saucepan.

4. Cut a 4-inch (10.25-cm) square of cheesecloth, and use twine to tie mixed pickling spice into a sachet. Add the sachet to vinegar mixture, and bring to a boil over high heat. Reduce heat to medium-low and simmer while you pack the jars.

5. Drain cucumbers in a colander, pressing gently to remove as much moisture as possible. Pack into prepared jars, leaving about $3/4$ inch (2 cm) headspace. Place 1 teaspoon black or yellow mustard seeds and 1 tablespoon dill seed into each jar.

6. Remove spice sachet from hot brine, and return brine to a boil. Pour over cucumbers, filling jars to $1/2$ inch (1.25 cm) headspace. Use a bubble remover to remove air bubbles by pressing gently around the cucumbers, and adjust headspace with more brine if necessary. Wipe rims and affix lids.

7. Process pint jars in a boiling-water canner for 10 minutes, then let the jars rest in the canner for 5 minutes before removing. Cool and store.

Sweet and Spicy Pickles

Thinly sliced cucumber and onion combine to create a pickle that's sweet with a spicy kick. This is my favorite quick pickle! Try them on burgers, sandwiches, or straight from the jar.

Yield: About 4 pints

4 lb. (1.75 kg) pickling (Kirby) cucumbers

1 medium red onion

3 TB. pickling salt

Ice

3¼ cups white vinegar

2¼ cups sugar

2 tsp. mixed pickling spice

¼ to ½ tsp. crushed red pepper flakes

1. Slice ⅛ inch (.25 cm) of blossom end off each cucumber, and discard. Slice cucumbers about ⅛ inch (.25 cm) thick using a mandoline, food processor, or sharp knife. Sprinkle cucumber slices with 1 tablespoon pickling salt, and cover with ice. Refrigerate and soak for 1 hour.

2. Stir remaining 2 tablespoons pickling salt, white vinegar, sugar, and mixed pickling spice in a medium saucepan over medium heat. Increase heat to high, bring to a boil, and then reduce heat to low and simmer while you pack the jars.

3. Drain cucumbers in a colander, pressing gently to remove as much moisture as possible. Pack into prepared jars, leaving about ¾ inch (2 cm) headspace.

4. Return brine to a boil. Pour over cucumbers, filling jars to ½ inch (1.25 cm) headspace. Use a bubble remover to remove air bubbles by pressing gently around cucumbers, and adjust headspace with more brine if necessary. Wipe rims and affix lids.

5. Process pint jars in a boiling-water canner for 10 minutes. Let the jars rest in the canner for 5 minutes, and then cool and store.

Pickled Green Beans

Everyone just loves these tart, slightly spicy pickles! Use a mix of green and yellow snap beans for a fun appearance.

Yield: About 4 pints

4 lb. (1.75 kg) green and yellow snap beans

1 tsp. crushed red pepper flakes

4 heads fresh dill

4 cloves garlic

$2^{1}/_{2}$ cups white vinegar

$2^{1}/_{2}$ cups water

$^{1}/_{4}$ cup canning salt

Snappy Solution

For a very crisp bean pickle, sterilize jars using the method outlined in Part 3, "Canning Food Basics," and process the green bean pickles for 5 minutes.

1. Wash green and yellow snap beans, and trim to fit in pint jars with $^{1}/_{2}$ inch (1.25 cm) headspace. Put $^{1}/_{4}$ teaspoon crushed red pepper flakes, 1 head fresh dill, and 1 garlic clove into each jar. Pack trimmed beans tightly into jars.

2. Bring white vinegar, water, and canning salt to a boil in a small saucepan over medium-high heat.

3. Pour canning liquid over beans, leaving $^{1}/_{2}$ inch (1.25 cm) headspace in jars. Use a bubble remover to remove air bubbles by pressing gently around beans, and adjust headspace with more pickling liquid if necessary. Wipe rims and affix lids.

4. Process pints in a boiling-water canner for 10 minutes. Turn off heat, remove the lid, and let jars stand in the canner for 5 minutes before removing. Cool and store.

Marinated Pickled Peppers

These peppers are, in a word, incredible. Use a mix of hot and sweet peppers to get them just the way you like them! I love to use a mix of sweet bell peppers and long hot Italian peppers.

Yield: About 9 half-pints

4 lb. (1.75 kg) mixed hot and sweet peppers

$1/4$ cup thinly sliced red onion

1 TB. dried oregano

1 cup bottled lemon juice

2 cups apple cider vinegar

2 TB. salt-packed capers, rinsed and drained (optional)

1 tsp. canning salt (optional)

2 to 3 cloves garlic, sliced

1 cup plus 2 TB. good-quality extra-virgin olive oil

1. Wash hot and sweet peppers well, and prick skin of each pepper a few times with a sharp paring knife. Roast under the broiler, on a hot grill, or over an open flame until skins are charred and blackened, turning frequently and monitoring constantly.

2. Place roasted peppers on a sheet pan or in a large bowl, cover tightly with plastic wrap, and let rest for 3 minutes. Slip the skins off peppers, remove cores and seeds, and set aside.

3. Bring red onion, oregano, bottled lemon juice, apple cider vinegar, salt-packed capers (if using), and canning salt (if using) to a boil in a small saucepan.

4. Stir peppers, sliced garlic, and extra-virgin olive oil in a large bowl, tossing to mix well.

5. Pack pepper mixture into hot half-pint jars, and then add hot pickling liquid to each jar, leaving $1/2$ inch (1.25 cm) headspace. Use a bubble remover to remove air bubbles by pressing gently around peppers, and adjust headspace with more pickling liquid if necessary. Wipe rims and affix lids.

6. Process jars in a boiling-water canner for 15 minutes. Turn off heat, remove the lid, and let jars stand in the canner for 5 minutes before removing. Cool and store.

Pickled Asparagus

If you like asparagus, you'll absolutely love it when it's pickled! Pickled asparagus also looks gorgeous in the jar, so it's a great choice for gift-giving to the pickle lovers in your life.

Yield: About 3 pints

4 lb. (1.75 kg) fresh asparagus

3 cloves garlic

1 1/2 tsp. dill seed

2 1/4 cups white vinegar

2 1/4 cups water

1/4 cup canning salt

1. Wash asparagus, and trim to fit in a pint jar (preferably wide-mouth) with 1/2 inch (1.25 cm) headspace. Put 1 garlic clove and 1/2 teaspoon dill seed into each hot, prepared jar. Pack asparagus tightly into jars.

2. Bring white vinegar, water, and canning salt to a boil in a small saucepan over medium-high heat. Pour canning liquid over asparagus, leaving 1/2 inch (1.25 cm) headspace in jars. Use a bubble remover to remove air bubbles by pressing gently around the asparagus, and adjust headspace with more pickling liquid if necessary. Wipe rims and affix lids.

3. Process pints in a boiling-water canner for 10 minutes. Turn off heat, remove the lid, and let jars stand in the canner for 5 minutes before removing. Cool and store.

Variation: For *Spicy Pickled Asparagus,* add 1 small hot chile pepper, halved (such as a Serrano pepper), to each jar.

Watermelon Rind Pickles

Watermelon-rind pickles are the eco- and budget-friendly pickle, since you're using the part of the watermelon that you'd ordinarily throw away! Watermelon rind becomes sweet, spicy, and crunchy when pickled. Serve them chilled for a refreshing treat.

Yield: About 4 to 5 pints

6 lb. (2.75 kg) watermelon rind

$^{3}/_{4}$ cup canning salt

2 qt. plus 3 cups water

Ice

9 cups granulated sugar

3 cups white vinegar

2 TB. mixed pickling spice

1 lime, seeded and thinly sliced

1. Pare hard, green skins and any red flesh from watermelon rinds, and cut into $^{1}/_{2}$-inch-wide (1.25 cm) strips that will fit in pint jars with $^{1}/_{2}$ inch (1.25 cm) headspace.

2. In a large bowl, stir canning salt into 2 quarts water until dissolved. Add watermelon rinds and ice to cover, refrigerate, and soak for 2 hours.

3. Drain watermelon, and place in a large pot with enough fresh water to cover. Bring to a boil over medium-high heat, and cook until tender, about 10 minutes.

4. Bring remaining 3 cups water, sugar, white vinegar, and mixed pickling spice (tied in cheesecloth, if desired) to a boil over medium-high heat in a large pot. Add watermelon rind and lime slices, and return to a boil. Reduce heat to low, and simmer for 1 hour.

5. Pack hot watermelon rinds in hot, prepared wide-mouth pint jars, and add canning liquid to each jar, leaving $^{1}/_{2}$ inch (1.25 cm) headspace. Use a bubble remover to remove air bubbles by pressing gently around the watermelon rind, and adjust headspace with more pickling liquid if necessary. Wipe rims and affix lids.

6. Process pints in a boiling-water canner for 10 minutes. Turn off heat, remove the lid, and let jars stand in the canner for 5 minutes before removing. Cool and store.

Peach Pickles

It sounds strange, but peaches make delicious pickles! Choose firm, slightly underripe peaches for the best results.

Yield: About 6 pints

8 lb. (3.5 kg) peaches

1 to 2 TB. whole cloves

6³/₄ cups granulated sugar

3 cups white or apple cider vinegar

3 sticks cinnamon, broken in half

6 star anise pods

1. Blanch peaches, dip in an ice bath, and remove skins. Halve and pit peaches, and treat to prevent browning (see "Preparing Fruits for Canning"). Drain peaches, and stick 1 clove into each half.

2. Bring sugar and white or apple cider vinegar to a boil in a large pot over medium-high heat, stirring to dissolve sugar.

3. Carefully place peaches in boiling syrup, and cook for 5 minutes. Skim foam if necessary after cooking.

4. Place ¹/₂ cinnamon stick and 1 star anise pod in each hot, prepared jar. Pack peaches and canning liquid into hot, prepared pint jars, leaving ¹/₂ inch (1.25 cm) headspace. Use a bubble remover to remove air bubbles by pressing gently around the peaches, and adjust headspace with more pickling liquid if necessary. Wipe rims and affix lids.

5. Process pints in a boiling-water canner for 20 minutes. Turn off heat, remove the lid, and let jars stand in the canner for 5 minutes before removing. Cool and store.

Pear Pickles

Anyone who has a pear tree (or knows someone who does) will look for new ideas for using all those delicious pears. How about pickles? These pears are simply spiced with cinnamon for a sweet-and-sour treat.

Yield: About 6 pints

8 lb. (3.5 kg) small pears (such as Seckel)

8 cups granulated sugar

4 cups white or apple cider vinegar

2 cups water

8 sticks cinnamon

2 TB. whole allspice

Packing Fruit Pickles

To minimize floating fruit, carefully pack hot peaches or pears into narrow-mouth pint jars. The "shoulders" of the jar will help hold down the fruit, leaving you with a pretty jar of fruit pickles.

1. Wash pears well, blanch for 30 seconds to loosen skins, and peel with a vegetable peeler. Halve pears, and use a melon baller to remove core. Treat to prevent browning (see "Preparing Fruits for Canning").

2. Bring sugar, vinegar, and water to a boil in a large pot over medium-high heat, stirring to dissolve sugar. Place allspice in a 4-inch (10.25-cm) square of cheesecloth, tie with twine, and add to canning syrup. Simmer 10 minutes.

3. Carefully place pears in boiling syrup, lower heat to medium-low, and simmer for 20 minutes. Skim if necessary after cooking.

4. Place 1 cinnamon stick in each hot, prepared jar. Remove spice bag, and pack pears and canning liquid into jars, leaving $1/2$ inch (1.25 cm) headspace. Use a bubble remover to remove air bubbles by pressing gently around the pears, and adjust headspace with more pickling liquid if necessary. Wipe rims and affix lids.

5. Process pints in a boiling-water canner for 20 minutes. Turn off heat, remove the lid, and let jars stand in the canner for 5 minutes before removing. Cool and store.

Making Fermented Foods

Fermented pickles and cabbage products are made by soaking cucumbers or cabbage in a brine until the lactic acid naturally present in these foods is released. Fermented products require a little more patience, but you'll be rewarded with a delicious pickled product that's good for your digestion.

What You'll Need

Jars or pickling crock

Vegetables

Mandoline, sharp knife, or food processor

Vinegar (if using)

Pot

Pickling or kosher salt

Filtered or distilled water

Spices (if using)

Zipper-lock bag

Pie plate

Kitchen towels

Before You Begin

1. Prepare jars
Wash jars or pickling crock in plenty of hot, soapy water. It is essential that picking vessels are perfectly clean and well-rinsed.

1. Wash

Wash vegetables in plenty of cold, running water. Choose recently harvested cucumbers, or fresh, firm, tightly packed heads of cabbage.

2. Trim

When canning cucumbers, cut off ⅛ inch (.25 cm) of the blossom end to prevent enzymes from softening pickles. When canning sauerkraut or kimchi, core cabbage before slicing.

3. Peel and slice

Cucumbers are normally fermented whole, but slice if you'll be eating them within a short period of time. Slice cabbage very thinly with a mandoline, sharp knife, or food processor. Peel radishes or carrots before slicing.

Using Kosher Salt

Kosher salt measures at twice the volume of canning salt, so you'll need to double the amount called for if you are using kosher rather than canning salt.

Choosing a Pickling Vessel

The fermented pickle recipes in this book can be prepared in either a 1-gallon (3.75-L) pickling crock or two or three quart-sized mason jars. To use a pickling crock, simply weight the pickles down with a clean plate and bag of brine. If you use canning jars, use narrow-mouth canning jars if possible, as the "shoulders" of the jars will help to keep the food submerged during fermentation. Weight the pickles with a small bag of brine, and place the inner part of the two-piece lid on loosely. In either case, keep canning vessels in a large pie plate or baking dish, as fermenting foods will occasionally bubble over (this is a sign that fermentation is occurring!).

4. Make brine (cucumber pickles)
Stir pickling or kosher salt into warm, filtered or distilled water in a pot, using the precise amounts directed in the recipe.

5. Fill jars
Pack vegetables tightly into jars or crock, leaving about 2 inches (5 cm) headspace to allow for fermentation. If making sauerkraut or kimchi, layer salt with cabbage to draw out liquid and create the brine.

6. Add brine to jars (cucumber pickles)
Reserving 1 cup brine for weight, pour brine into jars or crock, leaving about 2 inches (5 cm) headspace. Add spices, if using. Fill a zipper-lock bag with reserved brine, and place on top of mixture to keep pickles submerged.

7. Allow to ferment
You will see small bubbles as fermentation begins to occur.

Place jars in a pie plate, cover with a clean kitchen towel, and let stand at room temperature for approximately 3 days. If necessary, skim any foam or scum that rises to the top of the jar.

8. Store
Check periodically to see if the surface needs to be skimmed.

Taste to see if you like it. You can either cover it with a lid and store in the refrigerator or your cold storage room for up to 6 months or allow to ferment further at room temperature.

Processing Fermented Pickles

Processing fermented pickles destroys the beneficial enzymes created by the lactic acid fermentation process and results in softer pickles. If you want to reap the health benefits, you can just store them in the refrigerator for up to 6 months. If you wish to process pickles for long-term storage, add ¼ cup white vinegar to your brine once fermentation is complete, and process in a boiling-water canner, or, for crisper pickles, use this USDA-approved low-temperature pasteurization method.

1. Pack jars, leaving 1 inch (2.5 cm) headspace.

2. Fill a boiling-water canner halfway with water, and bring it to 120°F to 140°F (49°C to 60°C) over low heat. Bring a separate pot of water to a simmer over medium heat.

3. Wipe rims, seal jars, and place them in the canner. Then, add hot water to a level 1 inch (2.5 cm) above jars.

4. Increase heat to medium, and bring the water to exactly 180°F to 185°F (82°C to 85°C). Monitor constantly, raising or lowering heat if necessary, to maintain this temperature for 30 minutes.

Be sure to monitor the temperature of the water with a candy or jelly thermometer to be certain that a temperature of at least 180°F (82°C) is maintained during the entire 30-minute processing time. Temperatures higher than 185°F (85°C) may cause unnecessary softening of the pickles.

Kosher Half-Sour Pickles

Half sours are those delicious, crunchy pickles you find in big barrels at your favorite deli. When Kirby cucumbers are in season at my favorite local farm, I always have a crock of these in the refrigerator. Everyone sees them and wants to take some home, so they don't last long.

Yield: About 1 gallon (3.75 L)

4 lb. (1.75 kg) small green pickling cucumbers

8 cups filtered or distilled water

$1/2$ cup kosher salt

2 cloves garlic, peeled and halved (optional)

6 fresh dill heads or 3 TB. dill seed (optional)

2 TB. mustard seeds (optional)

1 TB. whole black peppercorns (optional)

1. Wash pickling cucumbers well, and slice $1/8$ inch (.25 cm) off blossom end of each cucumber. Leave pickles whole, or halve them. For crisp pickles, place cucumbers in a large bowl, cover with ice, refrigerate, and soak for 1 to 2 hours; drain.

2. Heat filtered or distilled water over medium-low heat in a saucepan until very warm but not boiling. Remove from heat, add kosher salt, and stir until salt is completely dissolved. Set aside to cool to room temperature.

3. Pack cucumbers tightly into jars. Add 2 cloves of garlic (if using), dill heads or dill seed (if using), mustard seeds (if using), and whole black peppercorns (if using).

4. Fill jars with brine so cucumbers are completely covered; save a little brine for weighting cucumbers. Weight cucumbers down with a saucer, and put a small plastic bag of reserved brine on top.

5. Lay a clean kitchen towel over jars, and let pickles sit out of direct sunlight in a cool place for about 3 to 4 days. After about 1 day, you will notice a little bubbling—that's fermentation in action. Check jars every day, and skim any foam or scum that has collected at the top.

6. Taste pickles after 3 days. At this point, you can store them in the refrigerator for up to 3 months or allow to ferment for a few more days before storing.

Variation: For *Jalapeño Half Sours,* add 1 sliced jalapeño pepper and 1 tablespoon coriander seeds to the brine. Do not can Jalapeño Half Sours.

Flavor Comes First!

I truly believe that canning fermented dill pickles ruins the flavor, texture, and health benefits of this delicious food. If you must can them, add ¼ cup white vinegar to the brine. Or for better results, make the Quick-Pack Dill Pickles earlier in this part.

Kimchi

This fiery fermented condiment is a staple in Korean cuisine. It's easy to make and safe to eat, as long as you follow the recipe precisely.

Yield: About 2 quarts

1 large Napa cabbage (about 4 lb. [1.75 kg]), cored and shredded

½ cup scallions, white and green parts, halved and roughly chopped

6 cloves garlic, peeled and thickly sliced

2 medium carrots, julienne cut

1 2-in. (5-cm) piece fresh ginger, peeled and julienne cut

¼ cup canning salt

1 tsp. sugar

1 to 2 TB. dried Korean chili powder, or to taste

1. Mix Napa cabbage, scallions, garlic, carrots, and ginger in a large bowl. Add canning salt and sugar, and thoroughly combine.

2. Pack mixture tightly into a fermenting crock or food-grade plastic or glass container with straight sides. Place a double layer of cheesecloth over mixture, followed by a clean, heavy plate. Top plate with a food-grade weight, such as a large Mason jar filled with water. In order for kimchi to ferment properly, it must be submerged in the liquid that will quickly form, so be sure your weight is heavy.

3. Allow mixture to stand at room temperature (around 70°F to 75°F [21°C to 24°C] is optimal) for 3 to 7 days. The progress of fermentation will be determined by the temperature in the room, so be patient. During the curing process, bubbles should form, generally after 3 to 4 days.

4. Taste kimchi mixture daily once fermentation has begun, and when it has reached your desired level of sourness (no more than 7 days), drain excess liquid, mix in Korean chili powder, and store in the coldest spot in your refrigerator for up to 30 days.

Sauerkraut

Sauerkraut has a distinct, sour cabbage flavor that is featured in many cuisines throughout eastern, central, and northern Europe.

Yield: About 2 quarts

5 lb. (2.25 kg) green cabbage (about 2 medium), shredded

¼ cup plus 1 TB. pickling salt

Helpful Hint

Processing sauerkraut in a boiling-water bath will end the fermentation process. If you store it in the refrigerator or in your cold storage room, fermentation will continue, although at a slower pace. Store unprocessed sauerkraut in crocks, or screw on two-piece lids loosely so the pressure does not build up in the jar.

1. Wash shredded green cabbage in several changes of cold water, and drain well. Thoroughly mix shredded cabbage and pickling salt.

2. Pack cabbage tightly with clean hands or a potato masher into a fermenting crock or food-grade plastic or glass container with straight sides. Place a double layer of cheesecloth over cabbage mixture, followed by a clean, heavy plate. Top plate with a food-grade weight, such as a heavy, well-sealed plastic bag filled with 1 quart water and 1 tablespoon pickling salt.

3. Allow mixture to stand in a cool place (around 68°F to 72°F [20°C to 22°C]) for 7 to 10 days. Once a day, tamp down cabbage mixture, ensuring it is well covered with brine. Skim any scum that forms on top of brine, and periodically wash cheesecloth and scald with boiling water. Keep cheesecloth moist by pouring 1 cup water mixed with 1 teaspoon pickling salt if it seems to be drying out.

4. When fermentation has occurred and sauerkraut tastes pleasingly sour, pack into sterilized glass jars along with fermentation liquid. Sauerkraut can be stored in the coldest part of the refrigerator for up to 2 months or canned in a boiling-water bath for 25 minutes. Either way, be sure to leave 1 inch (2.5 cm) headspace at the top of each jar to allow for expansion.

Preparing Relishes and Chutneys

Relishes and chutneys bring spice and zest to your table. Follow these easy steps to create delightful condiments featuring fresh produce and zingy spices.

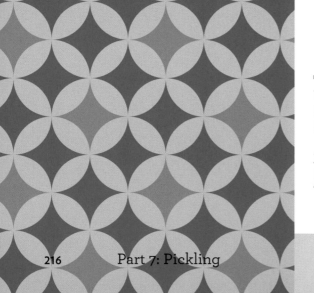

What You'll Need

Jars

Lids and seals

Canner

Treatment solution

Fruits

Vegetables

Peeler or paring knife

Ice bath (if needed)

Spices

Cheesecloth and kitchen twine

Saucepan

Sugar

Vinegar

Jar funnel

Bubble remover

Kitchen towels

Before You Begin

1. Prepare jars, lids, and canner
Prepare your jars, lids, and canner as outlined in "Preparing the Jars and Equipment." Keep jars and lids at a simmer until ready to use.

2. Prepare treatment solution
If you're using fruits or vegetables that need to be treated, see "Preparing Fruits for Canning" for detailed instructions.

1. Wash fruits and vegetables

Wash fruits and vegetables in plenty of cold, running water. Check for soft spots or blemishes.

2. Blanch, peel, and slice

Most fruits with peels, such as peaches and mangos, need to be peeled before canning. Use a vegetable peeler, or use the blanching/ice bath method outlined in "Preparing Fruits for Canning."

3. Treat fruit

Treat fruits that are prone to browning, such as peaches, apples, and pears, as soon as they are cut. Drain before proceeding.

Preparing Relishes and Chutneys

Cranberry-Apple Chutney

If you think you don't like chutney, you must try this sweet and not-too-spicy cranberry-apple version—it'll change your mind.

Yield: About 4 to 5 half-pints

1 lb. (453.5 g) fresh or frozen cranberries

1 cup apple cider vinegar

$1/2$ cup apple cider

$1^{1}/_{2}$ cups granulated sugar

1 cup finely chopped red onion

1 TB. grated fresh ginger

4 cups peeled, finely chopped apples

1 TB. mustard seeds

2 cinnamon sticks, broken in half

1 tsp. whole cloves

1 tsp. lightly crushed cardamom pods

1 tsp. whole black peppercorns

1. Combine cranberries, apple cider vinegar, apple cider, sugar, red onion, ginger, apples, and mustard seeds in a heavy-bottomed pot.

2. Place cinnamon sticks, cloves, cardamom pods, and black peppercorns in a 4-inch (10.25-cm) square of cheesecloth, and tie with kitchen twine to form a small spice bag.

3. Place the spice bag in the pot, and bring to a boil over medium-high heat. Reduce heat to low and simmer until chutney is thick and "jammy," stirring frequently, about 20 minutes.

4. Remove the spice bag. Pack chutney into hot, prepared jars with $1/2$ inch (1.25 cm) headspace. Use a bubble remover to remove any air by gently pressing around each jar. Check headspace and add more chutney to jars if necessary.

5. Process in a boiling-water canner for 10 minutes. At the end of the processing time, turn off the heat, and let the canner stand, uncovered, for 5 minutes. Remove jars to cooling racks or several layers of kitchen towels, and cool for 24 hours before checking seals and storing.

Mango Chutney

Mango is the classic Indian chutney. Serve it with Indian food, or use it as a delicious sandwich condiment or final flavor enhancement for soups and stews.

Yield: About 3 pints

5½ cups (about 6 mangoes) peeled, pitted, and chopped unripe mango

1 cup chopped sweet onion

½ cup chopped red bell pepper

1½ TB. grated fresh ginger

3 cloves garlic, finely chopped

2¼ cups granulated sugar

1½ cups apple cider vinegar

1¼ cups golden raisins

1 TB. mustard seeds

¾ tsp. canning salt

3 tsp. curry powder

1. Combine mango, sweet onion, red bell pepper, ginger, and garlic in a food processor, and pulse until very finely chopped but not completely puréed.

2. Mix sugar and apple cider vinegar in a large pot, and bring to a boil over medium-high heat. Stir until sugar is dissolved.

3. Add mango mixture, golden raisins, canning salt, mustard seeds, and curry powder, and bring to a boil over medium-high heat. Reduce heat to low and simmer, stirring frequently, until chutney is thick and "jammy," about 25 minutes.

4. Pack chutney into hot, prepared jars with ½ inch (1.25 cm) headspace. Use a bubble remover to remove any air by gently pressing around each jar. Check headspace and add more chutney to jars if necessary.

5. Process in a boiling-water canner for 10 minutes. At the end of the processing time, turn off the heat, and let the canner stand, uncovered, for 5 minutes. Remove jars to cooling racks or several layers of kitchen towels, and cool for 24 hours before checking seals and storing.

Hot Dog Relish

This classic, sweet-pickle hot dog topping gets its firm, gelled consistency from ClearJel, a commercial thickener that is also used in pie fillings.

Yield: About 4 to 5 half-pints

4 cups (about 2 large cucumbers) seeded, finely chopped cucumber

1 cup finely chopped onion

$^1/_2$ cup finely chopped red or green bell pepper

2 TB. canning salt

$1^1/_2$ tsp. ClearJel

$^1/_2$ cup apple cider vinegar

$^3/_4$ cup granulated sugar

$^1/_2$ tsp. celery seed

$^1/_4$ tsp. mustard seed

$^1/_4$ tsp. ground turmeric

$^1/_4$ tsp. ground nutmeg

1. Place cucumber, onion, and red or green bell pepper in a colander, and toss with canning salt. Drain for 2 to 3 hours, and then rinse and squeeze mixture to extract as much moisture as possible.

2. Whisk ClearJel and apple cider vinegar in a large saucepan until smooth. Add spices, and bring to a boil over medium-high heat.

3. Add drained vegetables, and bring back to a boil. Reduce heat to low and simmer for 10 minutes.

4. Pack relish into hot, prepared jars with $^1/_2$ inch (1.25 cm) headspace. Use a bubble remover to remove any air by gently pressing around each jar. Check headspace and add more relish to jars if necessary.

5. Process in a boiling-water canner for 10 minutes. At the end of the processing time, turn off the heat, and let the canner stand, uncovered, for 5 minutes. Remove jars to cooling racks or several layers of kitchen towels, and cool for 24 hours before checking seals and storing.

Sweet Onion Relish

Sweet onions and celery seed make a simple relish that's great for burgers and sandwiches.

Yield: About 4 half-pints

5 cups roughly chopped sweet white (such as Vidalia) or red onions

$1/2$ cup granulated sugar

1 cup white vinegar

1 TB. celery seed

1. Pulse sweet white or red onions in a food processor until very finely chopped but not completely puréed.

2. Mix chopped onions, sugar, white vinegar, and celery seed in a large saucepan, and bring to a boil over medium-high heat. Reduce heat to low and simmer for 10 minutes.

3. Pack relish into hot, prepared jars with $1/2$ inch (1.25 cm) headspace. Use a bubble remover to remove any air by gently pressing around each relish jar. Check headspace and add more relish to jars if necessary.

4. Process in a boiling-water canner for 10 minutes. At the end of the processing time, turn off the heat, and let the canner stand, uncovered, for 5 minutes. Remove jars to cooling racks or several layers of kitchen towels, and cool for 24 hours before checking seals and storing.

Corn Relish

Corn relish is so easy to make! Be sure your corn is sweet and freshly harvested. Corn relish is particularly delicious when served with grilled foods or fried green tomatoes.

Yield: About 4 to 5 half-pints

5 cups (about 8 ears) whole-kernel corn

2½ cups finely chopped red, green, and yellow bell peppers

1¾ cups finely chopped sweet onion

1¾ cups sugar

2½ cups apple cider vinegar (5 percent acidity)

4 tsp. canning salt

1¼ tsp. celery seed

1 TB. dry mustard

¾ tsp. turmeric

1. Combine corn; red, green, and yellow bell peppers; sweet onion; sugar; apple cider vinegar; canning salt; and celery seed in a large saucepan. Bring to a boil over medium-high heat, and cook for 4 minutes.

2. Ladle a little of cooking liquid into a small bowl, and whisk in dry mustard and turmeric. Return mustard mixture to the saucepan, and cook for 5 minutes.

3. Pack relish into hot, prepared jars with ½ inch (1.25 cm) headspace. Use a bubble remover to remove any air by gently pressing around each relish jar. Check headspace and add more relish to jars if necessary.

4. Process in a boiling-water canner for 10 minutes. At the end of the processing time, turn off the heat, and let the canner stand, uncovered, for 5 minutes. Remove jars to cooling racks or several layers of kitchen towels, and cool for 24 hours before checking seals and storing.

Sweet Pepper Relish

The only thing I can say about this sweet and slightly spicy relish is, "Try it." I promise you will love it.

Yield: About 4 half-pints

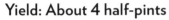

5 cups chopped red bell peppers

¾ cup chopped sweet red onion

1 cup granulated sugar

1¼ cups apple cider vinegar

1½ tsp. mustard seeds

½ tsp. crushed red pepper flakes

1. Pulse red bell peppers and sweet red onion in a food processor until very finely chopped, with an almost puréed consistency.

2. Mix chopped pepper-onion mixture, sugar, apple cider vinegar, mustard seeds, and crushed red pepper flakes in a large saucepan, and bring to a boil over medium-high heat. Reduce heat to low and simmer for 10 minutes.

3. Pack relish into hot, prepared jars with ½ inch (1.25 cm) headspace. Use a bubble remover to remove any air by gently pressing around each relish jar. Check headspace and add more relish to jars if necessary.

4. Process in a boiling-water canner for 10 minutes. At the end of the processing time, turn off the heat, and let the canner stand, uncovered, for 5 minutes. Remove jars to cooling racks or several layers of kitchen towels, and cool for 24 hours before checking seals and storing.

Part 8

Pressure Canning

Pressure canning is considered by many to be the Mount Everest of home food preservation. Pressure canning allows you to safely can low-acid foods by increasing the temperature at which food is processed. Modern pressure canners are safe and easy to use when you follow instructions and use tested methods. Read on to learn how to can low-acid foods at home.

Pressure Canning Basics

All low-acid foods (with a pH higher than 4.6) must be pressure canned. Boiling-water canners can reach a temperature of only 212°F (100°C), which is not high enough to eliminate botulism spores in low-acid foods. Pressure canners use steam to eliminate air, creating a pressurized environment in which the boiling water, steam vapor, and jars inside reach 240°F (116°C), safely eliminating all spoilers.

Foods That Need to Be Pressure Canned

Vegetables, most tomato-vegetable combinations, meats, fish, poultry, some fruit mixtures, and soups must all be processed in a pressure canner using up-to-date, tested methods. For best results, food should be pressure canned within a few hours of harvest.

Some vegetables will hold up better than others during pressure canning. For instance, spinach will clump together, making heat penetration unpredictable. Strong-tasting vegetables, such as rutabagas, become even stronger when pressure canned, producing undesirable flavors. Just because you *can* can a particular food does not necessarily mean you *should*. Consider the end result, and ask yourself whether you will want to eat the finished product, or whether another method will provide better results.

Before you begin pressure canning, though, review the safety and equipment lists in Part 3, "Canning Food Basics." Choose appropriate jars, two-piece lids, and field-fresh foods, and can only what you can handle within 2 to 3 hours, as the quality of the vegetables will deteriorate if left to stand at room temperature for too long.

Choosing a Pressure Canner

Pressure canners vary in price and quality and are available in dial-gauge and weighted-gauge models, both of which measure the amount of pressure required to hold a particular food at 240°F (116°C). Do not confuse pressure canners with pressure cookers—pressure cookers are cooking vessels that are not deep or heavy enough to safely can foods.

Use the following considerations to determine the pressure canner that is right for your budget and intended use:

Type of canner: *Dial-gauge canners* measure pressure using a gauge, which must be calibrated upon purchase (and each year thereafter) to be sure it is working properly. If a gauge is unpredictable by more than 1 pound (453.5 g) in either direction, it should be replaced. High readings can cause dangerous underprocessing, while low readings lead to overprocessing and quality issues.

Dial-gauge canners cannot vent air during processing, and some older models manufactured before 1970 have domed lids that can trap air inside. Consider having your canner evaluated for safety by your cooperative extension agent or government service organization if this type of pressure canner has been handed down through the years.

Weighted-gauge canners can be more expensive, but they control pressure more accurately by venting small amounts of steam and air each time the gauge rocks. Weighted-gauge canners require less "babysitting," as you can just listen for the rocking sound that indicates the correct pressure has been reached, rather than watching a gauge. They do not require yearly calibration.

Altitude Considerations

Those who live at higher altitudes may prefer a dial-gauge canner, as it is possible to adjust pressure. Weighted-gauge models can't be adjusted, and must always be operated at 15 pounds (6.75 kg) of pressure at higher altitudes, which can sometimes result in quality issues. See the altitude adjustment chart in "Using a Pressure Canner Safely" if you live at an altitude of 1,001 feet (305 m) or more above sea level.

Type of seal: All pressure canners must maintain an airtight seal to work properly. Some models use a lid gasket (also called a sealing ring), while others have a gasket-free, metal-on-metal seal. Pressure canners that seal with a gasket are less expensive than those with a gasket-free seal, but they also require more maintenance. The gasket must be inspected regularly, and replaced at least every 3 years, or sooner if it becomes hard, deformed, cracked, worn, or pitted. Gasket-free models are heavier and more expensive, but they last for generations and require little more than simple care of the seal according to the manufacturer's instructions. Before making an investment of several hundred dollars, consider how often you will use it, and determine your ongoing commitment to home canning. If you're in it for the long haul, a gasket-free model might be a good choice.

Weight: Lightweight, thin pots with a turn-on lid and gasket seal might be a better choice if you are petite or have back issues. Heavier canners, such as the deluxe gasket-free models discussed previously, are heavy to begin with. Once water is added, they can be very difficult for some people to lift.

Capacity: Pressure canner capacity is measured by the amount of water it will hold. A 21½-quart canner will hold 21½ quarts water and will process up to 7 quart jars or 19 pint jars (in two layers). The height of such a large canner may be an issue if you have an over-the-range microwave or if you are of small stature. The USDA recommends that a pressure canner hold at least 4 quart jars to be considered viable for pressure canning. The smaller canners, which hold only one layer of jars, might be a better choice if height or weight is an issue.

Stove type: Your cooking appliance also determines the type of canner you can use. For safe operation, the canner should have a circumference no more than 4 inches (10.25 cm) wider than your burner. Pressure canning on ceramic stovetops is not recommended, as the weight of the canner may crack the glass. Check with the manufacturer of your pressure canner before proceeding if you have a smooth-top range.

Pressure Canner Components and Maintenance

Taking proper care of your pressure canner is essential in order to keep it in proper working order for many years to come. Routine maintenance is essential for food safety, as well as your own safety, so don't skimp on the following steps!

Parts of a Pressure Canner

Read all instructions included with your pressure canner, check to be sure all parts are present, and wash and dry all parts before use. Make sure you also pay attention to the following:

- **Lid:** The lid should sit securely on the canner, making a tight-fitting seal. Do not submerge the dial gauge in water, and never attempt to wash it after use until it has cooled completely.

- **Gasket:** If your canner has a rubber gasket seal, be sure to wash and dry it. To keep it supple, lightly oil the gasket according to the manufacturer's instructions. Gaskets should be checked before each use and replaced every 3 years, or sooner if damaged. Never use a dried-out or cracked gasket.

- **Vent pipe:** Check to be sure the vent pipe is not clogged with dust, food, or grease. Hold it up to the light—you should be able to see through it.

- **Pressure regulator weight:** If you use a weighted-gauge canner, you will have a small weight that sits over the vent pipe. It is weighted for 5, 10, and 15 pounds (2.25, 4.5, and 6.75 kg) of pressure. After venting the canner, the dial gauge is set in place to bring the canner up to pressure.

- **Dial gauge:** If your canner has a dial gauge, have it checked yearly. You can call your local cooperative extension or government service organization for assistance. Never submerge the dial gauge in water, as this may set the gauge out of adjustment.

- **Pressure regulator (overpressure plug):** Check to be sure that the pressure regulator is not dried out, cracked, deformed, worn, pitted, or unusually soft, and replace if necessary, or every time you replace the rubber gasket. If pressure inside the canner reaches dangerous levels, the pressure regulator will vent steam by melting or lifting. Never use a pressure cooker after blowing the pressure regulator.

- **Petcock:** Dial-gauge canners have a petcock that's opened and closed to allow pressure to build and release. Check to be sure that the petcock is clear of obstructions before use.

- **Canning rack:** Wash and dry the canning rack between each use. Wrap it in newspaper and store it inside the canner between uses.

- **Base:** Wash and dry the base of your pressure canner between uses. If you have a cast-aluminum canner that becomes pitted, contact the manufacturer to see whether it is still safe to use.

Storing Your Pressure Canner

Improper storage will take years off the life of your canner. Store the canner in the box that it came in, or wrap the lid and all working parts in newspaper to keep dust out, and store them in a dry location. Before storing, clean your pressure canner, let it dry thoroughly, and lubricate gaskets or metal-on-metal seals according to the manufacturer's instructions.

Using a Pressure Canner Safely

Before you begin pressure canning, read all of the instructions in the manual provided with your canner and familiarize yourself with the processes and recipes you will be using. The following guidelines will help you to use your pressure canner safely.

Take It for a Spin

Before you start canning foods, it's helpful to do a "test run" with your canner to familiarize yourself with the process. Do a trial run with water only, using the manufacturer's instructions, to give yourself an idea of what to expect. That way, you'll know how long it takes for the canner to build pressure, see how your dial or weighted gauge works, and develop a better understanding of how long it will take to cool down. Going through the process with water only until you are comfortable will pay off—if you make a mistake or don't understand a particular process, the stakes are lower, and you won't lose a batch of food.

Be Prepared

The key to canning safely and successfully is preparation and organization. It's particularly important to read and understand your recipe—and the processes that you will be using to make it—before you begin.

Also, check to be sure all the equipment is in good working order. If it's your first project of the season, have your dial gauge tested to be sure it's in good working order, and replace any parts that are damaged or in poor condition.

Take the time to gather all equipment and food necessary before you get started. Plan to complete an entire project within a couple of hours, as allowing food to sit at room temperature, in or out of jars, for long periods of time will result in poor quality.

Adjust for Altitude

The canning process is affected by atmospheric pressures, which cause water to boil at lower temperatures. Therefore, it is essential to adjust for altitude when pressure canning if you live 1,001 or more feet (305 m) above sea level.

When adjusting for altitude using a pressure canner, refer to the following charts and read the instructions that came with your canner.

To adjust for altitude in pressure canners, increase pressure but not processing time. Adjust dial-gauge canners in 1-pound (453.5-g) increments depending on your altitude. Since a weighted-gauge canner cannot be adjusted in such small increments, always adjust a weighted-gauge canner by 5 pounds (2.25 kg) pressure at higher elevations.

Altitude Adjustments for Pressure Canning

Feet Above Sea Level	Dial-Gauge Canner	Weighted-Gauge Canner
0–1,000	11	10
1,001–2,000	11	15
2,001–4,000	12	15
4,001–6,000	13	15
Above 6,000	14	15

For more detailed information specific to your location, contact your county extension agent or your local government service organization.

Food	Processing Time (in Minutes)
Asparagus	Pints: 30
	Quarts: 40
Beans, shell, and field peas	Pints: 75
	Quarts: 90
Beans, snap	Pints: 20
	Quarts: 25
Carrots	Pints: 25
	Quarts: 30
Corn kernels	Pints: 55
	Quarts: 85
Greens	Pints: 70
	Quarts: 90
Mushrooms, cultivated (whole or sliced)	Half-pints or pints: 45
Okra	Pints: 25
	Quarts: 40
Peas, green (shelled)	Pints or quarts: 30
Potatoes, sweet (cubed only)	Pints: 65
	Quarts: 90
Potatoes, white	Pints: 35
	Quarts: 40
Pumpkin or winter squash (cubed only)	Pints: 55
	Quarts: 90

For more information on these adjustments, read the instructions that came with your canner, and contact your county extension agent or local government service organization.

Take Care!

Always observe the following precautions when pressure canning:

- Lubricate the seals (both gasket and metal on metal) before use. See the manufacturer's instructions for specific information.

- Keep safety openings clear by checking the valves, vents, and weights frequently to ensure that steam can pass through them.

- Use the right amount of water. Follow the manufacturer's recommendations for the amount of water required for your canner.

- Never allow the canner to boil dry—this will destroy your canner, and it will have to be replaced. Check in between batches, and replenish the water if you are using the canner multiple times in one day. Never use a canner that has been boiled dry.

- Don't drop your canner. If you do drop it, return it to the manufacturer for examination, or ask your county extension agent or local government service organization to inspect it for damage before using it.

- Never leave your pressure canner unattended! You must be present to monitor the pressure and adjust the heat if the pressure becomes too high or too low.

- Maintain steady temperatures. Don't move your pressure canner from a cold storage room directly to a hot burner in a warm room. Allow the canner a few hours at room temperature to avoid warping the metal and ruining your canner.

- Never submerge your hot canner in cold water. Allow the canner to cool gradually, as a rapid loss of pressure will make canned foods unsafe for consumption.

- Handle with care. Always use heavy oven mitts to prevent burns, and be sure that pressure has dropped completely before you open your canner. Refer to the instruction booklet for your canner.

- Most pressure canners can be used as pressure cookers, too. However, never use your pressure cooker to cook foods that foam and froth—such as rice, pasta, beans, applesauce, cranberries, or rhubarb—as foaming foods can clog vent pipes, creating unsafe conditions. When using your canner as a pressure cooker, never fill it more than halfway. Be vigilant about cleaning as well, as fats and starches can clog valves.

- Avoid canning pumpkin or squash purées. They are too viscous for home canning, and tested methods have not been developed that allow for proper heat penetration. Pumpkin and winter squash may be canned in chunks, with plenty of liquid, using tested and approved recipes.

Don't Bite Off More Than You Can Chew

I can't tell you how many budding home canners simply burn themselves out. Pace yourself to stay in the game; don't expect to process 100 pounds (45.25 kg) of berries or 3 bushels of tomatoes in a single weekend. Work in reasonably sized batches. After all, you don't need 50 jars of jam.

Steps for Pressure Canning

Follow all steps precisely for safe pressure canning. It seems like quite a bit of work, but it only takes a few minutes to ensure your safety as well as the quality and safety of the food you'll be canning. Do this every time for safe and accurate results.

What You'll Need

Pressure canner

Jars

Lids and seals

Canning rack

Saucepan

Jar lifter

Jar funnel

Ladle

Bubble remover or plastic butter knife

Paper towel or kitchen towel

Magnetic lid lifter

1. Examine pressure canner

See "Pressure Canner Components and Maintenance" for details.

Examine all parts, replacing any that are damaged. Be sure the dial gauge has been tested recently, if necessary.

2. Examine jars

Look for scratches or chips. Recycle damaged jars.

3. Examine lids and bands

Use new lids every time. Check the rubber seals to be sure they are not cracked or brittle. Discard lids that are dented, misshapen, or have gaps in the rubber seal. Bands may be reused many times. Discard bands that are dented or rusted.

4. Wash equipment and jars

Wash the equipment and jars in hot, soapy water, and dry them with a clean, lint-free dish cloth. It is not necessary to sterilize jars when pressure canning.

Not Too Hot!

Many canners are not recommended for use on burners that put out more than 12,000 British Thermal Units (BTU) of heat. If you have a stove with high-output burners, check your manufacturer's recommendations before use to prevent damage to your canner. If you have a professional-type stove, consider investing in a heavier, professional grade cast-aluminum model.

5. Fill the canner

Fill with hot water using the amount recommended by the manufacturer, or 2 to 3 inches (5 to 7.5 cm) of water if not specified. Center the canner on your stove's largest burner.

6. Insert rack and add empty jars

An instant-read thermometer is helpful for this task.

Heat water and jars to 140°F (60°C) for raw pack or 180°F (82°C) for hot pack. When the water reaches the right temperature, reduce the heat to hold a steady temperature while you prepare the food.

7. Place lids in saucepan

Place lids in a small saucepan with warm water, and bring to a simmer for 10 minutes, and then keep hot until you fill the jars with food. Never boil lids.

8. Prepare food

Use a tested recipe to prepare food for pressure canning.

9. Fill jars

Remove hot jars from the canner with a jar lifter, and use a jar funnel and ladle to fill the jars with hot food.

10. Remove bubbles

Use a bubble remover or a plastic butter knife to gently remove air pockets and bubbles from the food.

11. Check and adjust headspace

Use the notched end of your bubble remover to check headspace—it's marked for this purpose. Adjust headspace after bubbling, if necessary.

12. Wipe jar rims

A perfectly clean rim is essential for a proper seal, so use hot water and a clean paper towel or kitchen towel to wipe the rim of each jar.

13. Affix lids

Use a magnetic lid lifter to fish lids out of simmering water. Affix lids on clean jar rims, and tighten screw bands to fingertip tightness.

14. Place jars in canner

If necessary, adjust hot water in your canner to equal the recommended amount, or 2 to 3 inches (5 to 7.5 cm), and return to a simmer. Use a jar lifter to carefully place jars in canner.

15. Affix canner lid

Follow the manufacturer's instructions to secure the lid of your canner.

16. Increase temperature and vent steam

Raise the heat to high to bring the water inside the canner to a boil. When a boil is reached, steam will flow freely from the open vent pipe. The USDA recommends you allow steam to exhaust from your canner for 10 minutes to remove all air and build pressure. Set a timer.

17. Close petcock or set weight

If you are using a dial-gauge canner, close the petcock after 10 minutes of venting. If you are using a weighted-gauge canner, set the weight to the desired pressure.

18. Bring canner up to pressure

For a dial-gauge canner, monitor the gauge closely to bring the canner up to pressure. For a weighted-gauge canner, the weight will begin to rock at regular intervals once pressure is achieved.

19. Set a timer

When the canner reaches the appropriate level of pressure, set a timer for the precise amount of time specified in the recipe.

20. Monitor heat and pressure

Raise or lower heat setting to maintain proper pressure. If pressure drops more than 1 pound (453.6 g) below the recommended setting at any point, or the weights stop rocking, restore pressure and begin timing again for the full amount of processing time.

21. Turn off heat and allow pressure to drop

Never submerge the canner in cold water.

Turn off the heat, and allow the canner to cool and pressure to drop. For a dial-gauge canner, let the canner sit undisturbed until the gauge reaches zero, and then open the petcock. For weighted-gauge models, allow the canner to stand undisturbed for the period of time recommended by the manufacturer.

22. Remove lid

After the pressure has reached zero, wait 10 minutes before opening the lid. Wearing oven mitts, cautiously loosen the lid. Remove the lid slowly away from you, and set on a heatproof surface.

23. Remove jars

Use a jar lifter to remove jars from the canner, and place them 1 inch (2.5 cm) apart on a folded towel or cooling rack, keeping them upright at all times.

24. Let jars stand

For more information on cooling and storing jars, refer to Part 3, "Canning Food Basics."

Let jars stand undisturbed for 24 hours. Check the seals, and then store in a cool, dry place away from sunlight.

Pressure Canning Troubleshooting

Before consuming any canned food, it is important to inspect it for spoilage and to handle the food properly before serving. Signs of spoilage include loose or bulging lids, leaks, off odors, mold, foam, and bubbling or spurting liquid. If any of these signs is present, dispose of the food safely (see "Identifying and Disposing of Spoiled Food" for detailed instructions).

Power Failure

If electricity or gas is lost during pressure canning, do the following:

- If power is restored quickly and the jars are still warm, reprocess the jars for the entire time specified in the recipe.
- If it's not possible to reprocess the jars immediately, store them at 40°F (4°C) up to overnight. Replace the lids with new, unused lids, and reprocess for the entire time specified in the recipe.
- If power or gas will be out for several days, try to reprocess the jars at another location, remove food from jars and freeze instead, or cook and consume immediately.

Jars Did Not Seal

Canned foods can be reprocessed within 24 hours if the jar did not seal during processing. Generally, this step is only worthwhile if an entire batch fails to seal. If a single jar does not seal, freeze the contents, or cook and eat immediately.

To reprocess jars, determine the reason for failure. If an entire batch fails to seal, it's most likely that the seals on the lids were old or faulty. Remove the lid and inspect the sealing rim of the jar. If the jar itself is not defective, readjust the headspace, wipe the sealing edge, and affix a *new* two-piece lid (remember to simmer the lid first to soften the seal). If just a few seals have failed, you may not need new screw bands. Inspect them to be sure they are *true* (perfectly round), and replace if necessary. Reprocess the jars for the entire amount of time recommended in the recipe.

Safe Preparation of Pressure-Canned Foods

In addition to obvious signs of spoilage, it is important to be vigilant about botulism, which is undetectable in many cases. Look for bulging lids, spurting liquid, or seal failure. Always be certain that your pressure canner is in good working order, and that you have followed all recommendations for sanitation, food selection, and processing exactly.

Loss of Liquid in Jars

Loss of liquid in jars, or *siphoning,* is not in itself an indication of spoilage. Liquid loss can occur for any of the following reasons. If no other signs of spoilage are present, it is safe to consume.

- **Rapid loss of pressure:** This is when reduction of pressure in the canner is forced. Do not subject the canner to temperature changes, such as putting it in a cold place, or open the pressure valve before the pressure reaches zero.
- **Fluctuating pressure:** For safety and quality, it's essential to maintain steady pressure during the entire processing time.
- **Air bubbles and pockets in jar:** Remove all air pockets with a bubble remover before processing.
- **Food packed too tightly, or improper headspace:** Follow instructions to the letter, and measure headspace before sealing jars.
- **Poor seal:** Use new lids every time, and tighten bands to fingertip tightness—not too loose, not too tight.
- **Improper preparation of starchy vegetables:** Make sure that beans, squash, and potatoes are cooked until tender without overcooking before canning, so they do not absorb extra liquid.

Cloudy Liquid in Jars

Cloudy liquid can be a sign of spoilage. The following factors can cause cloudy liquid. Use common sense, and discard food properly if any other signs of spoilage are present.

- **Starchy vegetables:** Choose vegetables that are perfectly ripe or just underripe. Mature or overripe vegetables are a poor choice for canning.
- **Poor choice of canning medium:** Pack starchy vegetables in boiling water, not cooking liquid, to avoid excess starch.
- **Minerals in water:** If you have hard water, choose distilled or softened water for canning.
- **Additives in salt:** Choose additive-free salt, such as canning, pickling, or kosher salt.

Sediment in Jars

Sediment on its own is not necessarily a sign of spoilage. Sediment can occur from an excess of starch in vegetables, additives in salt, or hard water. When canning some vegetables, sediment formation is natural. For example, spinach will form white crystals, while onions and green vegetables often form yellow sediment. As long as no other signs of spoilage are present, the food is safe to consume.

Precautions for Eating Pressure-Canned Foods

Always follow these safety precautions when consuming canned low-acid foods:

- Never taste food before heating.
- Bring canned foods to a boil in a saucepan and boil for 10 minutes, or reduce heat and simmer for 15 minutes.
- Do not heat pressure-canned foods in a microwave. The uneven heat can leave cold spots.
- If preparing casseroles or baked dishes from canned goods, cook until the temperature of the food reaches 185°F (85°C) on an instant-read thermometer.

Save Those Jars!

A jar that is cloudy or scaly may be salvageable. Try soaking scaly, cloudy, or film-covered jars in a solution of 1 cup 5 percent acidity white vinegar to 1 gallon (3.75 L) water for 2 to 3 hours. Wash jars, and examine for damage. Jars that are cared for properly can last for many years.

Canned Green Beans

Canned green beans have excellent flavor, and retain many of their vital nutrients. Green (snap) beans will yield about a quart for every 2 pounds (907 g) beans, and a pint for every pound.

Adjustments for Altitude

If you live at an altitude above 1,001 feet (305 m), refer to "Using a Pressure Canner Safely" for important information about altitude adjustment for all pressure canning recipes.

Yield: About 7 quarts or 9 pints

For 7 qt.: 14 lb. (6.25 kg) plump, tender green beans

For 9 pt.: 9 lb. (4 kg) plump, tender green beans

Boiling water

Kosher or canning salt (optional)

1. Inspect green beans. Discard any that are spoiled, rusty, or shriveled.

2. Snap ends off green beans, and cut into 1-inch (2.5-cm) pieces if desired.

3a. *Hot-pack method:* Place green beans in a large pot, and cover with boiling water. Boil for 5 minutes, and then loosely fill hot jars with beans and cooking liquid, leaving 1 inch (2.5 cm) headspace.

3b. *Raw-pack method:* Fill hot jars tightly with raw green beans. Cover with boiling water, leaving 1 inch (2.5 cm) headspace.

4. Add 1 teaspoon kosher or canning salt to each quart jar or ½ teaspoon to each pint jar (if using).

5. Remove bubbles and air pockets with a bubble remover, and adjust headspace with more boiling water or hot cooking liquid if necessary. Wipe jar rims, affix two-piece canning lids, and screw bands to fingertip tightness.

6. Process according to the following chart. Cool and store.

Style of Pack	Hot or raw
Canner Pressure	Dial gauge: 11 PSI
	Weighted gauge: 10 PSI
Processing Time (in Minutes)	Pints: 20
	Quarts: 25

Italian-Style Green Beans with Tomatoes

Tomatoes and green beans make a delicious combination, accented with a touch of onion, basil, and oregano.

Yield: About 9 pints

8 lb. (3.5 kg) plump, tender green beans

2 lb. (907 g) plum tomatoes, peeled, seeded, and diced

1 cup onion, diced

1 tsp. dried basil

$\frac{1}{2}$ tsp. dried oregano

$4\frac{1}{2}$ tsp. canning salt (optional)

1. Inspect green beans. Discard any that are spoiled, rusty, or shriveled.

2. Snap ends off beans, and cut into 1-inch (2.5-cm) pieces if desired.

3. Combine green beans, plum tomatoes, and onion in a large pot with enough water to cover, and stir in basil and oregano. Bring to a boil, and cook for 5 minutes.

4. Add $\frac{1}{2}$ teaspoon canning salt to each jar (if using). Pack mixture and cooking liquid loosely in hot jars, leaving 1 inch (2.5 cm) headspace.

5. Remove bubbles and air pockets with a bubble remover, and adjust headspace with more boiling water or hot cooking liquid if necessary. Wipe jar rims, affix two-piece canning lids, and screw bands to fingertip tightness.

6. Process in a dial-gauge pressure canner at 11 PSI for 75 minutes or a weighted-gauge canner at 15 PSI for 90 minutes. Cool and store.

For Safety's Sake

When canning mixed vegetables, it's important to have plenty of water in the mix. The best description I've ever heard is that the mix should be "sloppy" to produce safe results. Some of the liquid can be drained before eating.

Asparagus

Choose tender asparagus spears with tight tips for best results. The raw-pack method is the best choice for whole asparagus spears.

Yield: About 7 quarts or 9 pints

For 7 qt.: 24½ lb. (11 kg) fresh asparagus
For 9 pt.: 16 lb. (7.25 kg) fresh asparagus
Boiling water
Canning salt (optional)

1. Wash asparagus. Snap off tough ends, and use a vegetable peeler to peel lower half of asparagus spears. Trim spears to fit jars with the appropriate headspace, or cut into 1-inch (2.5-cm) pieces.

2a. *Hot-pack method:* Place sliced asparagus in a large pot, and cover with boiling water. Boil for 5 minutes, and then loosely fill hot jars with asparagus and cooking liquid, leaving 1 inch (2.5 cm) headspace.

2b. *Raw-pack method:* Fill hot jars tightly with trimmed raw asparagus spears. Cover with boiling water, leaving 1 inch (2.5 cm) headspace.

3. Add 1 teaspoon canning salt to each quart jar or ½ teaspoon to each pint jar (if using).

4. Remove bubbles and air pockets with a bubble remover, and adjust headspace with more boiling water or hot cooking liquid if necessary. Wipe jar rims, affix two-piece canning lids, and screw bands to fingertip tightness.

5. Process according to the following chart. Cool and store.

Style of Pack	Hot or raw
Canner Pressure	Dial gauge: 11 PSI
	Weighted gauge: 10 PSI
Processing Time (in Minutes)	Pints: 30
	Quarts: 40

Carrots

Carrots can beautifully. They retain their color and flavor well and are great to have on hand for soups, side dishes, and casseroles.

Yield: About 7 quarts or 9 pints

For 7 qt.: 17½ lb. (8 kg) fresh carrots, without tops

For 9 pt.: 11 lb. (5 kg) fresh carrots, without tops

Boiling water

Canning salt (optional)

1. Wash and peel carrots, and then rinse under cold water. Slice or chop as desired. Do not can whole carrots.

2a. *Hot pack method:* Place carrots in a large pot, and cover with boiling water. Boil for 5 minutes, and then loosely fill hot jars with carrots and cooking liquid, leaving 1 inch (2.5 cm) headspace.

2b. *Raw-pack method:* Fill hot jars tightly with carrot pieces. Cover with boiling water, leaving 1 inch (2.5 cm) headspace.

3. Add 1 teaspoon canning salt to each quart jar or ½ teaspoon to each pint jar (if using).

4. Remove bubbles and air pockets with a bubble remover, and adjust headspace with more boiling water or hot cooking liquid if necessary. Wipe jar rims, affix two-piece canning lids, and screw bands to fingertip tightness.

5. Process according to the following chart. Cool and store.

Style of Pack	Hot or raw	
Canner Pressure	Dial gauge: 11 PSI	
	Weighted gauge: 10 PSI	
Processing Time (in Minutes)	Pints: 25	
	Quarts: 30	

Dried Beans or Field Peas

When you compare the cost of store-bought canned beans to dry beans that you cook and can yourself, it's easy to see that canning your own dried beans and field peas is both convenient and economical.

Yield: About 7 quarts or 9 pints

For 7 qt.: 5 lb. (2.5 kg) dried beans or field peas
For 9 pt.: 3½ lb. (1.5 kg) dried beans or field peas
Cold water
Boiling water
Canning salt (optional)

1. In a large pot with cold water to cover, soak beans or field peas overnight. Drain and rinse, discarding soaking water.

2. Place beans or field peas in a large stock pot with water to cover. Bring to a boil over medium-high heat, and cook for 30 minutes.

3. Add 1 teaspoon canning salt to each quart jar or ½ teaspoon to each pint jar (if using).

4. Loosely fill jars with beans or field peas and cooking liquid, leaving 1 inch (2.5 cm) headspace.

5. Remove bubbles and air pockets with a bubble remover, and adjust headspace with more boiling water or hot cooking liquid if necessary. Wipe jar rims, affix two-piece canning lids, and screw bands to fingertip tightness.

6. Process according to the following chart. Cool and store.

Style of Pack	Hot or raw
Canner Pressure	Dial gauge: 11 PSI
	Weighted gauge: 10 PSI
Processing Time (in Minutes)	Pints: 75
	Quarts: 90

Beans with Tomato-Molasses Sauce

Can your own "baked beans" with this easy recipe. These sweet and saucy beans are terrific on their own, or you can add your favorite flavorings, such as bacon or mustard, before heating.

Yield: About 7 quarts or 9 pints

For 7 qt.: 5 lb. (2.5 kg) dried beans or field peas

For 9 pt.: 3½ lb. (1.5 kg) dried beans or field peas

Cold water

1 qt. home-canned tomato juice

3 TB. dark molasses

2 tsp. canning salt

1 TB. finely chopped onion

1 TB. apple cider vinegar

1 tsp. dried mustard

1. In a large pot with cold water to cover, soak beans or field peas overnight. Drain and rinse, discarding soaking water.

2. Place beans or field peas in a large stock pot with water to cover. Bring to a boil over medium-high heat, and cook for 30 minutes. Drain and discard cooking liquid.

3. When beans or field peas are nearly done cooking, combine tomato juice, dark molasses, canning salt, onion, apple cider vinegar, and dried mustard in a saucepan. Bring to a boil over medium-high heat, and cook for 5 minutes.

4. Loosely fill hot jars ¾ full with beans or field peas, and then fill with hot tomato-molasses sauce, leaving 1 inch (2.5 cm) headspace.

5. Remove bubbles and air pockets with a bubble remover, and adjust headspace with more boiling water or hot cooking liquid if necessary. Wipe jar rims, affix two-piece canning lids, and screw bands to fingertip tightness.

6. Process according to the following chart. Cool and store.

Style of Pack	Hot or raw
Canner Pressure	Dial gauge: 11 PSI
	Weighted gauge: 10 PSI
Processing Time (in Minutes)	Pints: 65
	Quarts: 75

Whole-Kernel Corn

Canned corn makes a quick side dish for supper or can be used as an ingredient in soups, casseroles, and corn bread.

Yield: About 7 quarts or 9 pints
  For 7 qt.: 31½ lb. (14.25 kg) fresh sweet corn (in husks)
  For 9 pt.: 20 lb. (9 kg) fresh sweet corn (in husks)
  Cold water
  Boiling water
  Canning salt (optional)

1. Husk sweet corn, and carefully remove silk. Wash well.

2. In a large pot with plenty of boiling water, blanch whole corn cobs for 3 minutes. Cool quickly in an ice bath.

3. Use a sharp knife or corn cutter to remove kernels from cobs, cutting only ¾ of the way through depth of kernels.

4a. *Hot pack method:* In a large pot, add 1 cup boiling water for each clean quart or pint of corn kernels. Boil for 5 minutes, and loosely fill hot jars with cooking liquid, leaving 1 inch (2.5 cm) headspace.

4b. *Raw-pack method:* Loosely fill hot jars with raw corn kernels, taking care not to shake or press down on kernels. Add fresh boiling water, leaving 1 inch (2.5 cm) headspace.

5. Add 1 teaspoon canning salt to each quart jar or ½ teaspoon to each pint jar (if using).

6. Remove bubbles and air pockets with a bubble remover, and adjust headspace with more boiling water or hot cooking liquid if necessary. Wipe jar rims, affix two-piece canning lids, and screw bands to fingertip tightness.

7. Process according to the following chart. Cool and store.

Style of Pack	Hot or raw
Canner Pressure	Dial gauge: 11 PSI
	Weighted gauge: 10 PSI
Processing Time (in Minutes)	Pints: 55
	Quarts: 85

Cream-Style Corn

Cream-style corn has a smoother consistency, and can be used any way you would use whole-kernel corn. Its increased viscosity means a longer processing time.

Safely Canning Cream-Style Corn

To ensure safety, cream-style corn should be processed only in pint jars. If you use larger jars, heat penetration will not be sufficient to eliminate dangerous spoilers.

Yield: About 9 pints

20 lb. (9 kg) fresh sweet corn (in husks)
Water for cooking and processing
4$\frac{1}{2}$ tsp. canning salt (optional)

1. Husk sweet corn, and carefully remove silk. Wash well.

2. In a large pot with plenty of boiling water, blanch whole corn cobs for 4 minutes. Cool quickly in an ice bath.

3. Use a sharp knife or corn cutter to remove kernels from cobs, cutting about halfway through depth of kernels. Use the flat side of your knife to scrape the remaining corn and liquid from cobs.

4. Add 2 cups boiling water for each clean pint of corn kernels. Bring to a boil, and loosely fill hot jars with cooking liquid, leaving 1 inch (2.5 cm) headspace.

5. Add canning salt to each pint jar (if using).

6. Remove bubbles and air pockets with a bubble remover, and adjust headspace with more boiling water or hot cooking liquid if necessary. Wipe jar rims, affix two-piece canning lids, and screw bands to fingertip tightness.

7. Process according to the following chart. Cool and store.

Style of Pack	Hot or raw
Canner Pressure	Dial gauge: 11 PSI
	Weighted gauge: 10 PSI
Processing Time (in Minutes)	Pints: 85

Peas: Green or English

Canned peas will not have the same "snap" and freshness as frozen peas, but if freezer space is at a premium, canning will retain most of the nutrients and yield a good-tasting side dish or recipe ingredient.

Yield: About 7 quarts or 9 pints

For 7 qt.: 31$^1\!/_2$ lb. (14.25 kg) unshelled green peas
For 9 pt.: 20 lb. (9 kg) unshelled green peas
Boiling water
Canning salt (optional)

1. Wash green pea pods. Discard any discolored or diseased pods. Shell, and then wash peas again under plenty of running water.

2a. *Hot-pack method:* Place shelled peas in a large pot, and cover with boiling water. Boil for 2 minutes, and then loosely fill hot jars with peas and cooking liquid, leaving 1 inch (2.5 cm) headspace.

2b. *Raw-pack method:* Fill hot jars with raw peas. Cover with boiling water, leaving 1 inch (2.5 cm) headspace.

3. Add 1 teaspoon canning salt to each quart jar or $^1\!/_2$ teaspoon to each pint jar (if using).

4. Remove bubbles and air pockets with a bubble remover, and adjust headspace with more boiling water or hot cooking liquid if necessary. Wipe jar rims, affix two-piece canning lids, and screw bands to fingertip tightness.

5. Process according to the following chart.

Style of Pack	Hot or raw
Canner Pressure	Dial gauge: 11 PSI
	Weighted gauge: 10 PSI
Processing Time (in Minutes)	Pints: 40
	Quarts: 40

Mushrooms: Whole or Sliced

It is safe to can domestically grown button mushrooms. Look for small, firm specimens at your farmers' market with unopened caps. Canned mushrooms are delicious when drained and sautéed with a little garlic and olive oil or added to pasta sauce. Pack mushrooms in pint or half-pint jars only.

Yield: About 1 pint for every 2 pounds (907.25 g) mushrooms

5 pt. or 10 half-pt.: 10 lb. (4.5 kg) fresh button mushrooms

Cold water

Canning salt (optional)

Ascorbic acid (optional)

1. Soak mushrooms in cold water for 10 minutes to remove soil. Drain and rinse well. Leave small mushrooms whole; halve and quarter larger specimens.

2. Place mushrooms in a saucepan with water to cover. Bring to a boil over medium-high heat, and cook for 5 minutes.

3. Add ½ teaspoon canning salt and ⅛ teaspoon ascorbic acid to each pint or half-pint jar (if using). Pack mushrooms and liquid, leaving 1 inch (2.5 cm) headspace.

4. Remove bubbles and air pockets with a bubble remover, and adjust headspace with more boiling water or hot cooking liquid if necessary. Wipe jar rims, affix two-piece canning lids, and screw bands to fingertip tightness.

5. Process according to the following chart.

Style of Pack	Hot or raw
Canner Pressure	Dial gauge: 11 PSI
	Weighted gauge: 10 PSI
Processing Time (in Minutes)	Pints: 45

Lima Beans

Look for plump pods that contain green lima beans. Canned lima beans are delicious, and they retain their texture well after canning. Try feeding them to the lima bean haters in your family, and see if you change a few minds!

Yield: About 7 quarts or 9 pints

For 7 qt.: 28 lb. (12.75 kg) unshelled lima beans

For 9 pt.: 18 lb. (8.25 kg) unshelled green peas

Boiling water

Canning salt (optional)

1. Wash lima bean pods. Inspect and discard any discolored or diseased pods. Shell, and then wash lima beans again under plenty of running water.

2a. *Hot-pack method:* Place shelled peas in a large pot, and cover with boiling water. Boil for 2 minutes, and then loosely fill hot jars with lima beans and cooking liquid, leaving 1 inch (2.5 cm) headspace.

2b. *Raw-pack method:* Fill hot jars with raw lima beans, taking care not to press or pack beans down, and cover with boiling water. For small beans, leave 1 inch (2.5 cm) headspace for pints and 1$\frac{1}{2}$ inches (3.75 cm) headspace for quarts. For large beans, leave 1 inch (2.5 cm) headspace for pints and 1$\frac{3}{4}$ inches (4.5 cm) headspace for quarts.

3. Add 1 teaspoon canning salt to each quart jar or $\frac{1}{2}$ teaspoon to each pint jar (if using).

4. Remove bubbles and air pockets with a bubble remover, and adjust headspace with more boiling water or hot cooking liquid if necessary. Wipe jar rims, affix two-piece canning lids, and screw bands to fingertip tightness.

5. Process according to the following chart. Cool and store.

Style of Pack	Hot or raw
Canner Pressure	Dial gauge: 11 PSI
	Weighted gauge: 10 PSI
Processing Time (in Minutes)	Pints: 40
	Quarts: 50

Succotash

Fresh lima beans and corn mix with homemade crushed tomatoes to make up this classic side dish. As with all vegetable mixes, the processing time is significantly longer.

Yield: About 7 quarts

15 lb. (6.75 kg) fresh sweet corn, in husks
14 lb. (6.25 kg) fresh lima beans, in pods
2 qt. canned crushed tomato sauce
Boiling water
7 tsp. canning salt (optional)

1. Wash and husk sweet corn, and carefully remove silk. Cut kernels off each cob, slicing about $3/4$ of the way through the depth of the kernels. Wash, shell, and rinse lima beans.

2. In a large pot with enough boiling water to cover, combine sweet corn, lima beans, and canned crushed tomato sauce. Bring the mixture to a boil over medium-high heat, and cook for 5 minutes.

3. Loosely fill hot jars with succotash, evenly distributing liquids and solids and leaving 1 inch (2.5 cm) headspace.

4. Add 1 teaspoon canning salt to each jar (if using).

5. Remove bubbles and air pockets with a bubble remover, and adjust headspace with more boiling water or hot cooking liquid if necessary. Wipe jar rims, affix two-piece canning lids, and screw bands to fingertip tightness.

6. Process according to the following chart. Cool and store.

Style of Pack	Hot or raw	
Canner Pressure	Dial gauge: 11 PSI	
	Weighted gauge: 10 PSI	
Processing Time (in Minutes)	Pints: 60	
	Quarts: 85	

Potatoes

The best potatoes for canning are firmer varieties, such as Yukon gold. Canned potatoes are perfect for mashing or adding to soups and casseroles.

Yield: About 7 quarts or 9 pints

For 7 qt.: 20 lb. (9 kg) potatoes
For 9 pt.: 13 lb. (6 kg) potatoes
Ascorbic acid
Boiling water
Canning salt (optional)

1. Wash and peel potatoes, trimming away any dark or discolored spots and rinsing with plenty of cold running water.

2. To prevent potatoes from darkening, place each peeled, rinsed potato in a solution of citric or ascorbic acid (1 teaspoon to 1 gallon [3.75 L] water). If desired, cut each potato into $1/2$-inch (1.25-cm) chunks.

3. Drain potatoes, and place in a large pot with boiling water to cover by several inches. Bring to a boil, and cook for 10 minutes. Drain and discard cooking water.

4. Fill hot jars loosely with cooked potatoes, and then add fresh boiling water, leaving 1 inch (2.5 cm) headspace.

5. Add 1 teaspoon canning salt to each quart jar or $1/2$ teaspoon to each pint jar (if using).

6. Remove bubbles and air pockets with a bubble remover, and adjust headspace with more boiling water or hot cooking liquid if necessary. Wipe jar rims, affix two-piece canning lids, and screw bands to fingertip tightness.

7. Process according to the following chart. Cool and store.

Style of Pack	Hot or raw
Canner Pressure	Dial gauge: 11 PSI
	Weighted gauge: 10 PSI
Processing Time (in Minutes)	Pints: 35
	Quarts: 40

Sweet Potatoes

Sweet potatoes can be canned in boiling water or in heavy syrup. If you'd like to use syrup, turn to Part 4, "Canning Fruits and Pie Fillings," for syrup preparation instructions.

Yield: About 7 quarts or 9 pints

For 7 qt.: 17½ lb. (8 kg) sweet potatoes
For 9 pt.: 11 lb. (5 kg) sweet potatoes
Boiling water
Boiling water or medium syrup
Canning salt (optional)

1. Wash sweet potatoes, and boil in a saucepan or steam in a vegetable steamer set in 1 inch (2.5 cm) water for 20 minutes over medium heat until nearly cooked but still firm. Peel and cut into uniform chunks. Discard cooking liquid.

2. Fill hot jars loosely with sweet potato chunks, and then add fresh boiling water or syrup, leaving 1 inch (2.5 cm) headspace.

3. Add 1 teaspoon canning salt to each quart jar or ½ teaspoon to each pint jar (if using).

4. Remove bubbles and air pockets with a bubble remover, and adjust headspace with more boiling water or hot cooking liquid if necessary. Wipe jar rims, affix two-piece canning lids, and screw bands to fingertip tightness.

5. Process according to the following chart. Cool and store.

Style of Pack	Hot
Canner Pressure	Dial gauge: 11 PSI
	Weighted gauge: 10 PSI
Processing Time (in Minutes)	Pints: 65
	Quarts: 90

Peppers

This method can be used for any type of hot or sweet pepper. Be sure to wear gloves when handling hot peppers!

Yield: About 9 pints

9 lb. (4 kg) sweet or hot peppers
Boiling water
4½ tsp. canning salt (optional)

1. Peel peppers by blistering the skins under the broiler, over the flame on your stovetop, or on a hot barbecue grill.

2. Place peppers on a baking sheet, and cover tightly with plastic wrap. Cool for several minutes, and then uncover and peel.

3. Remove cores and seeds. Leave small peppers whole; slice larger peppers into two or three sections.

4. Flatten peppers, and pack loosely in hot pint jars, taking care not to press or pack. Cover with fresh boiling water, leaving 1 inch (2.5 cm) headspace.

5. Add ½ teaspoon canning salt to each jar (if using).

6. Remove bubbles and air pockets with a bubble remover, and adjust headspace with more boiling water or hot cooking liquid if necessary. Wipe jar rims, affix two-piece canning lids, and screw bands to fingertip tightness.

7. Process according to the following chart. Cool and store.

Style of Pack	Hot or raw
Canner Pressure	Dial gauge: 11 PSI
	Weighted gauge: 10 PSI
Processing Time (in Minutes)	Pints: 35

Greens

Try canning a variety of sturdy cool-weather greens, such as mustard or kale—try any combination of greens, such as beet, turnip, chard, or collards.

Canning Spinach

Spinach is a tender green and may develop an undesirably soft consistency after canning. In addition, oxalates in spinach bind with other elements and crystallize, forming white sediment in the jars. While it is safe to eat, some find canned spinach unsightly.

Yield: About 7 quarts or 9 pints

For 7 qt.: 28 lb. (12.75 kg) freshly harvested greens
For 9 pt.: 18 lb. (8.25 kg) freshly harvested greens
Boiling water
Canning salt (optional)

1. Wash greens thoroughly in several changes of cold water.

2. Plunge greens into a large bowl filled with plenty of water, swish them around, and then lift out. Discard water, and repeat the process until no grit, soil, or sand is left in water.

3. Examine greens carefully, and discard any that are wilted or discolored. Cut out any tough stems or ribs.

4. Steam 1 pound (453.5 g) greens at a time in a vegetable steamer set over a few inches boiling water in a large saucepan for 3 to 5 minutes, until wilted. Pack greens loosely in hot jars, taking care not to press or pack down. Fill with fresh boiling water, leaving 1 inch (2.5 cm) headspace.

5. Add ½ teaspoon canning salt to each quart jar or ¼ teaspoon to each pint jar (if using).

6. Remove bubbles and air pockets with a bubble remover, and adjust headspace with more boiling water or hot cooking liquid if necessary. Wipe jar rims, affix two-piece canning lids, and screw bands to fingertip tightness.

7. Process according to the following chart. Cool and store.

Style of Pack	Hot or raw
Canner Pressure	Dial gauge: 11 PSI
	Weighted gauge: 10 PSI
Processing Time (in Minutes)	Pints: 70
	Quarts: 90

Stewed Tomatoes

Stewed tomatoes and other tomato-vegetable mixtures should be pressure canned for safety.

Yield: About 6 pints or 3 quarts

12 lb. (5.5 kg) plum or paste tomatoes, blanched, peeled, cored, and chopped (see Part 6, "Canning Tomatoes and Tomato Products")

1 cup celery, chopped

$1/2$ cup onion, chopped

$1/4$ cup green or red bell pepper, seeded and chopped

1 TB. granulated sugar

2 tsp. canning salt

1. In a large pot over medium heat, combine plum or paste tomatoes, celery, onion, green or red bell pepper, sugar, and canning salt. Cover and bring to a boil. Simmer for 10 minutes, stirring once or twice.

2. Ladle hot tomato mixture into hot jars, leaving 1 inch (2.5 cm) headspace.

3. Remove bubbles and air pockets with a bubble remover, and adjust headspace if necessary. Wipe jar rims, affix two-piece canning lids, and screw bands to fingertip tightness.

4. Process according to the following chart. Cool and store.

Style of Pack	Hot or raw	
Canner Pressure	Dial gauge: 11 PSI	
	Weighted gauge: 10 PSI	
Processing Time (in Minutes)	Pints: 15	
	Quarts: 20	

Spaghetti Sauce

If you have a pressure canner, you can put up a delicious Italian-style spaghetti sauce. Once you try this, you'll never go back to store-bought!

Yield: About 9 pints

30 lb. (13.5 kg) plum or paste tomatoes, blanched, peeled, seeded, and quartered (see Part 6, "Canning Tomatoes and Tomato Products")

¼ cup extra-virgin olive oil

1 cup finely chopped onion

4 cloves garlic, very finely chopped

½ cup finely chopped celery

½ cup finely chopped red bell pepper

1 lb. (453.5 g) fresh button or cremini mushrooms, thinly sliced

4½ tsp. kosher or canning salt

2 tsp. dried oregano

2 tsp. dried basil

1. Place tomatoes in a large pot, and bring to a boil over medium-high heat. Boil for 20 minutes, stirring frequently.

2. Heat extra-virgin olive oil in a large sauté pan over medium-high heat. Add onion, garlic, celery, red bell pepper, and button or cremini mushrooms, and cook, stirring occasionally, until tender, about 10 minutes.

3. Run tomatoes through a food mill or sieve to purée. Return to the pot, and stir in sautéed vegetables, canning salt, oregano, and basil. Bring to a boil over high heat. Reduce heat to medium-low and simmer until volume is reduced by half.

4. Pack spaghetti sauce in hot jars, leaving 1 inch (2.5 cm) headspace.

5. Remove bubbles and air pockets with a bubble remover, and adjust headspace with more boiling water or hot cooking liquid if necessary. Wipe jar rims, affix two-piece canning lids, and screw bands to fingertip tightness.

6. Process according to the following chart. Cool and store.

Style of Pack	Hot
Canner Pressure	Dial gauge: 11 PSI
	Weighted gauge: 10 PSI
Processing Time (in Minutes)	Pints: 20

Appendix A

Glossary

anaerobic   Literally translated, "without air." Canning processes take place in an anaerobic environment, as processing removes air from the canning vessel.

ascorbic acid   Commonly known as vitamin C, used in powder form to prevent browning in fruits and vegetables.

blanch   To place a food in boiling water for about 1 minute or less to partially cook the exterior, and then submerge in or rinse with cool water to halt the cooking.

blend   To completely mix something, usually with a blender or food processor; slower than beating.

boil   To heat a liquid to the point where water is forced to turn into steam, causing the liquid to bubble. To boil something is to insert it into boiling water. A rapid boil is when a lot of bubbles form on the surface of the liquid.

boiling-water canning   The process of preserving food by heating jars in boiling water.

brine   A highly salted, often seasoned liquid used to flavor and preserve foods. To brine a food is to soak or preserve it by submerging it in brine.

brining   To soak food in a brine solution.

calcium citrate   A salt of citric acid that is used as a preservative. *See* citric acid.

Campylobacter   A pathogenic bacterium that can cause foodborne illness.

canning   The practice of preserving food by heating it in specially designed jars and lids using either a boiling-water bath or pressure canner.

canning salt   A pure salt without additives, such as iodine, minerals, or anticaking agents. Using canning salt prevents cloudiness or discoloration in pickled foods.

case hardening   A condition that occurs when dehydrated foods are prepared at too high a temperature, causing the outside to dry prematurely and trap moisture within. Case-hardened foods are not safe to eat.

check   Pretreatment method in which the skins of fruit are either blanched or pierced to ensure even drying.

chiffonade   Method of finely shredding leaf vegetables or herbs, which are stacked, rolled, and sliced.

chop   To cut into pieces, usually qualified by an adverb such as "coarsely chopped" or by a size measurement such as "chopped into 1/2-inch pieces." "Finely chopped" is much closer to minced.

chutney   A thick condiment often served with Indian curries made using fruits or vegetables with vinegar, sugar, and spices.

cider vinegar   A vinegar produced from apple cider that's popular in North America.

citric acid   A sharp-tasting crystalline acid present to some degree in almost all foods. Citric acid is used in canning and preserving to increase acidity and inhibit microbial growth.

Clostridium botulinum   An anaerobic, pathogenic, spore-forming bacterium that produces the toxin botulin, which causes the potentially deadly disease botulism.

Clostridium perfrigens   An anaerobic, pathogenic, spore-forming bacterium that is widely distributed in the environment and is the most common cause of foodborne illness in the United States.

cornstarch   A thickener used in baking and food processing. It's the refined starch of the endosperm of the corn kernel and often mixed with cold liquid to make into a paste before adding to a recipe to avoid clumps.

cure   To preserve uncooked foods by either salting and smoking or pickling them.

dehydrating   A food preservation process that removes moisture from food to allow for long-term storage.

double boiler   A set of two pots designed to nest together, one inside the other, and provide consistent, moist heat for foods that need delicate treatment. The bottom pot holds water (not quite touching the bottom of the top pot); the top pot holds the food you want to heat.

enzymes   Substances produced by all living organisms. In canning, enzymes participate in important food preservation reactions, and can also contribute to spoilage.

Escherichia coli (E. coli)   A bacterium commonly found in the digestive systems of humans and other animals. Some rare strains of *E. coli* can produce verotoxin, a cause of serious foodborne illness.

extract   A concentrated flavoring derived from foods or plants through evaporation or distillation that imparts a powerful flavor without altering the volume or texture of a dish.

fermentation   A process that produces lactic acid to preserve food.

food mill   A hand-cranked preparation utensil for puréeing and straining soft foods.

foodborne illness   Diseases caused by consuming food or water contaminated with pathogenic microorganisms.

freezer burn   Spoilage of frozen foods caused by exposure to air.

fresh-pack pickles   Unfermented pickles packed in a vinegar solution and preserved in a boiling-water bath.

GRAS (Generally Recognized as Safe)   An acronym used by the United States Food and Drug Administration (USDA) to denote a food additive that is recognized by experts as safe for its intended use.

handful   An unscientific measurement, it's the amount of an ingredient you can hold in your hand.

headspace   Space left at the top of a container when canning or freezing food, to allow for expansion and to maintain a proper seal.

hot pack   A method of packing cooked foods into hot jars with hot liquid before processing.

hull   The removal of the calyx (or hull) of a fruit, such as strawberries.

infusion   A liquid in which flavorful ingredients, such as herbs, have been soaked or steeped to extract their flavor into the liquid.

kosher salt   A coarse-grained salt made without any additives or iodine.

lactic acid bacteria   A group of bacteria that contribute to the fermentation of many products, such as pickles, sauerkraut, kimchi, and wine. Lactic acid bacteria increase the acidity of foods, inhibiting the growth of pathogens and extending shelf life.

lacto-fermentation   Fermentation caused by lactic acid bacteria.

Listeria monocytogenes   A pathogenic bacterium that can cause serious foodborne illness in people at high risk, such as children, the elderly, or immune compromised. It resists chilling, freezing, drying, and heating.

mandoline   A kitchen tool with an adjustable blade that creates uniform, thin slices of food.

mince   To cut into very small pieces, smaller than diced, about 1/8 inch or smaller.

olive oil   A fragrant liquid produced by crushing or pressing olives. Extra-virgin olive oil—the most flavorful and highest quality—is produced from the first pressing of a batch of olives. Other olive oils are also produced from later pressings.

oxidation   The browning of fruit flesh that happens over time and with exposure to air. Minimize oxidation by rubbing the cut surfaces with lemon juice.

paprika   A rich, red, warm, earthy spice that lends a rich red color to many dishes.

pasteurization   Partial sterilization of foods at a temperature that destroys harmful microorganisms without causing changes to the physical quality of the food.

pectin   A soluble carbohydrate that is present to some degree in all fruits that's used as a setting agent in jams and jellies.

phytonutrients   Unique, protective compounds present in all plants that act as antioxidants in the body.

pickling   The process of preserving food using a combination of acid, salt, and/or fermentation.

pickling salt   *See* canning salt.

pickling spice   A combination of whole spices used to flavor pickled vegetables.

pine nut   A nut that's rich (high in fat), flavorful, and a bit pine-y. Pine nuts are a traditional ingredient in pesto and add a hearty crunch to many other recipes.

pith   The bitter white membrane located beneath the peel of citrus fruits.

Pounds per Square Inch (PSI)   A measurement of atmospheric pressure. At sea level, water boils at 212°F (100°C). By increasing the pressure, water boils at a higher temperature.

pressure canning   A canning method that increases the amount of PSI (pressure per square inch) in the canning vessel to 240°F (115°C), allowing for safe processing of low-acid foods.

purée   To reduce a food to a thick, creamy texture, typically by using a blender or food processor.

reduce   To boil or simmer a broth or sauce to remove some of the water content, resulting in more concentrated flavor and color.

reserve   To hold a specified ingredient for another use later in the recipe.

rosemary   A pungent, sweet herb used with chicken, pork, fish, and especially lamb. A little goes a long way.

sage   An herb with a musty yet fruity lemon-rind scent and "sunny" flavor.

Salmonella   A pathogenic bacterium that can cause foodborne illness from a variety of foods when products are improperly handled or incompletely cooked.

savory   1. A popular herb with a fresh, woody taste. 2. Used to describe the flavor of food (the opposite of sweet).

scant   An ingredient measurement directive not to add any extra, perhaps even leaving the measurement a tad short.

shelf-stable products   Foods that can be safely stored at room temperature.

simmer   To boil gently so the liquid barely bubbles.

skim   To remove fat or other material from the top of a liquid.

sodium chloride   Common salt, which is available in many forms, including table salt, canning salt, kosher salt, and sea salt.

Staphylococcus   A pathogenic bacterium that causes foodborne illness. It can be controlled by proper food handling and good sanitation practices.

steam   To suspend a food over boiling water and allow the heat of the steam (water vapor) to cook the food. This quick-cooking method preserves a food's flavor and texture.

steep   To let sit in hot water, as in steeping tea in hot water for 10 minutes.

stew   To slowly cook pieces of food submerged in a liquid. Also, a dish prepared by this method.

tarragon   A sweet, rich-smelling herb perfect with seafood, vegetables (especially asparagus), chicken, and pork.

thyme   A minty, zesty herb.

vegetable steamer   An insert with tiny holes in the bottom designed to fit on or in another pot to hold food to be steamed above boiling water. *See also* steam.

vinegar   An acidic liquid widely used as a dressing and seasoning, often made from fermented grapes, apples, or rice. When canning, use only commercially prepared vinegar with an acidity of 5 percent. *See also* cider vinegar; white vinegar.

whisk   To rapidly mix, introducing air to the mixture.

white vinegar   The most common type of vinegar, produced from grain.

wine vinegar   Vinegar produced from red or white wine. Wine vinegar is not commonly used in home canning.

yeast   Tiny fungi that, when mixed with water, sugar, flour, and heat, release carbon dioxide bubbles, which in turn cause the bread to rise.

zest   Small slivers of peel, usually from a citrus fruit, such as a lemon, lime, or orange.

Appendix B

References and Further Reading

I encourage you to seek out new recipes, research, and ideas, as canning is an eternal learning process. I recommend the following books and websites.

Books

Andress, Elizabeth, and Judy Harrison. *So Easy To Preserve.* Georgia: University of Georgia Cooperative Extension Service, 2006.

Bone, Eugenia. *Well-Preserved.* New York: Clarkson Potter, 2009.

Cancler, Carole. *The Home Preserving Bible.* Indiana: Alpha Books, 2012.

Kingry, Judi. *Ball Complete Book of Home Preserving.* California: Robert Rose, 2006.

Virant, Paul. *The Preservation Kitchen: The Craft of Making and Cooking with Pickles, Preserves, and Aigre-doux.* California: Ten Speed Press, 2012.

Online Resources

Ball Canning: freshpreserving.com

Cornell University Cooperative Extension: cce.cornell.edu

Food in Jars: foodinjars.com

Foodpreserving.org: www.foodpreserving.org

HOMEGROWN.org: homegrown.org

National Center for Home Food Preservation: nchfp.uga.edu

Punk Domestics: punkdomestics.com

United States Department of Agriculture: usda.gov

Index

Photography by Kevin Bertolacci, with the following exceptions:

3, 12, 68, 69, 134, 191   William Reavell © Dorling Kindersley

4   Deepak Aggarwal © Dorling Kindersley

4   Peter Gardner © Dorling Kindersley

4   Sarah Ashun © Dorling Kindersley

4   Tina Rupp © Dorling Kindersley

5, 12, 70   Howard Shooter © Dorling Kindersley

5   Masterfile

6, 7, 13   Used with permission from Whirlpool Corporation

8, 49   Steve Gorton © Dorling Kindersley

12   Andy Crawford and Steve Gorton © Dorling Kindersley

13   Andy Crawford © Dorling Kindersley

27   Peter Anderson © Dorling Kindersley

32, 33   Charles Schiller © Dorling Kindersley

33   David Henley © Dorling Kindersley

45   Simon Smith © Dorling Kindersley

47   Francesca Yorke © Dorling Kindersley

55   Jeremy Hopley © Dorling Kindersley

70   Roger Phillips © Dorling Kindersley

70   Ruth Jenkinson © Dorling Kindersley

71   Dave King © Dorling Kindersley